BEING GLORIFIED
TOGETHER WITH HIM

BEING GLORIFIED TOGETHER WITH HIM

The Reward of the Inheritance

Charlie Dines

While this 2013 edition contains some minor word modifications of the original 2012 edition, its overall content and theme remain unchanged.

A large majority of the scriptural excerpts in this writing are eclectic renderings reflecting my understanding of what the passage is intending to say based on carefully reviewing more than one dozen English translations of the Bible (KJV, NKJV, NIV, NASB, ASV, RV, ISV, LITV, Webster Bible, Weymouth N.T., YLT, ESV, EMTV, TLB, Darby, NLT, TEV, RecV) and several Greek texts. Being persuaded of their right rendering as they appear herein—and praying that the Lord will not find them to be any wresting of His Word—I have not included any version references throughout this writing. It is left to the reader to consult the Word of God for himself to become satisfied of their correctness.

Within Scripture citations, non-bracketed italics represent words implied or supplied by the translators, or words that appear in a Greek text but not in English translations. Bracketed italics are the author's added notations; they are no part of Holy Writ. Some words appear in regular, bracketed type: e.g., "[Christ]" where the text says "He," the textual reference being to Christ; or where "anyone" or "he" within the context means "[a believer]"; or where "you" is replaced by "[we]" in order to make the verse more relevant to the Christian reader.

ISBN-13: 978-1475006483
ISBN-10: 1475006489

Cover design was the cooperative effort of:
   Eric Baker, Springfield, MO: contact <beprinting@sbcglobal.net>
   Wendy Richard, Portland, OR: contact <wendylanay@gmail.com>

Author contact: cdines6@gmail.com

Dedication

To all who will pursue the reward of the inheritance.

Table of Contents

Appendices

Acknowledgments

This section is a most important one to me as the writer, for I am well aware of how certain ones have contributed to this book's ever having been written.

Above all others, I wish to recognize my wife, Ione, who was willing to be left nearly a widow for two years while I was studying, writing, proofreading, and revising these writings. Thank you, my Love. Your patient endurance with me during our many years together must surely await its reward in that Day of His appearing.

For over three decades David Culver has been a mentor to me. Would that every Christian was so blessed to have an older, more spiritually exercised saint in his life to help guide him along the way. I will be forever indebted to you, David.

Every believer needs certain, special companions in faith with whom he can have regular fellowship. In addition to David—and though there have been many others—I must single out a few with whom I have spent countless hours in fellowship at different times. Their names are Craig Rogers, Greg McVay (Gregger, to me), Gary Hipp, and Hulon Champlin. Many of their thoughts and comments, and even their occasionally taking umbrage with certain of my views, have had a most positive influence on my continued musings in the Word of God. Thank you, brethren.

My profound gratitude is extended to Lewis Schoettle for having persevered in publishing and distributing certain doctrinal books into a niche market among Christians. The works available through his publishing firm[1] have been of inestimable value to me. Thank you, Lewis, for your faithful continuance in the work that the Lord has assigned to you.

Finally, I offer what is, in most cases, a posthumous thank you to so many Christian authors, too numerous to record herein. These writers are or were of various doctrinal bents, their works having helped to lead me along into an understanding of the way of God more perfectly (Acts 18.26).

Thank you all.

---

[1] Schoettle Publishing Co., Inc. (pronounced "shuttle"), P.O. Box 1246, Hayesville, NC, 28904; web site <www.schoettlepublishing.com/>; phone contact 706/896-3333.

An Allegory

Two lads, living in the squalor of a foreign orphanage, are noticed by a certain man who has come to that place looking to acquire sons for himself. From among so many, he takes pity on these two wretched souls—who knows why? He pays the fee required and takes them unto himself, giving them his own name. They are now his heirs.

As it happens, their adoptive father is a man of great means, and these two sons stand to inherit a fortune. But besides his personal treasure, he has created a concern that has worldwide influence. He invites both sons to come to work with him, assuring them that he will provide all of the knowledge and understanding required for them to become successful in his present and future enterprises.

Only one of the brothers seizes upon the opportunity, diligently seeking to be fruitful in his father's business. The other son goes about life according to his own self-interests, being complacent in the comforts of his new circumstances and in the assuredness of his future inheritance.

In the end of things, this latter son will receive only what was warranted to him from the start, while the other son will ultimately inherit a double portion of wealth and intimacy with his father—plus authority over his father's affairs.

Preface

"Jesus…have mercy on me!"

This was the loud, public pleading of the blind beggar, Bartimaeus, nearly two millennia ago. While his pitiful cries annoyed Jesus' disciples, He opened this blind man's eyes to see Him (Mark 10.46ff).

Perhaps someone who is not a Christian has happened upon this book and decided to read its first few pages. To him or her I have devoted Chapter 1. I pray that your eyes may be opened to see the wonders of the Lord Jesus, and the salvation from sin and eternal life that are to be found only in Him.

All of the remaining chapters should be of particular interest to believers.

My purposes in writing this book are threefold. First, since my childhood in the '40s and '50s I have observed the world changing dramatically. Troubled societies worldwide are advancing quickly into unimaginable financial, political, moral and social chaos; and mankind is destitute of solutions despite any (political) claims to the contrary.

Being now an older man, I have a great concern for my children and my children's children who may well live into those dreadful days ahead. My heartfelt hope is that they may become strong in the faith of Jesus Christ as the days darken. I pray that those future days will find them all numbered among those who will be able to lift their heads and look up as their redemption draws near (Luke 21.28).

Secondly, this writing is intended to bring into view the hope of our calling as Christians. Believers in this present day are being misled concerning this glorious hope. It is a hope about which we hear little of in the preachings and teachings of our day. This was not the case in the early Church.

Thirdly, I intend to support the truth that the means by which men live their lives now will bear irrevocably upon the eternal destiny of each, including Christians. For those who may read this book to its conclusion, I pray that you might come out the other end a changed person, with a clear understanding of God's high calling in Christ Jesus. May we all put aside any façade, any erroneous teachings, any unfit speech and behavior, and even the lethargy that may have become the portion of some while wandering in a spiritual desert.

My overall purpose throughout this writing is borrowed from another: "To humble the pride of man, to exalt the grace of God in salvation, and to promote real holiness in heart and life."[1]

Excepting some things appearing in the Appendices and certain footnotes, I have made every effort to avoid being too technical, praying that this writing will be comprehensible, convincing, and compelling to every ordinary reader. Many references to Scripture are included throughout this writing to support its teachings.

My intentions in writing echo the remarks made by the apostle Peter in his second epistle.

> 2 Pet. 1.12-15   Therefore, I intend to always be ready to remind you of these things... 13 I consider it right, as long as I am in this earthly dwelling, to stir you up by way of reminder, 14 knowing that the laying aside of my earthly dwelling is imminent, as also our Lord Jesus

---

[1]   This purpose statement has appeared on the cover of quarterly publications of "Free Grace Broadcaster" for many years. These booklets are most profitable to read, and they may be obtained free of charge by contacting Chapel Library's website: www.mountzion.org.

Christ has made clear to me. 15 Moreover, I will be diligent, so that at any time after my departure you may be able to recall these things.

While I have many nice tools and farm equipment, and some fine fishing gear, and boxes of blessed books to be passed on to others, I have nothing of more value to leave behind than this writing. I pray that it will stir you up.

Perhaps this might be a good time to pause to read my personal testimony in Appendix C (page 175) before moving on, so that you may have the opportunity of becoming better acquainted with me as the author.

May the Lord bless you in the course of your reading this labor of love.

Charlie Dines
Marshfield, MO
2012

"Come Now, Let Us Reason Together"

(Isa. 1.18)

When they unjustifiably nailed Jesus to a cross, why didn't He exercise His power and save Himself? He had the power, and He had demonstrated it by doing many miracles, even raising the dead.

This question thrust itself upon my consciousness half a lifetime ago. Back then it was one for which I could find no answer. If you are not presently a believer in the good news concerning Jesus Christ, and the forgiveness of sin and salvation to be found in Him, I invite you to inquire of yourself: "Why didn't Jesus save Himself in order to prove to His enemies who He is?"

In this chapter you will discover the answer.

The Bible is the Very Word of God

Many people protest, "The Bible is just some book written by mere men," even though they may have never studied one iota of Holy Writ. Others, who may have read portions of it from Genesis through Revelation, claim, "It contains many errors."

Although apparent inconsistencies can be reconciled through more meticulous study, these critics hold fast to their false assumptions for one reason: to become convinced of the truths of the Bible would cause them to know that they are accountable to their Creator, life-Sustainer, and Judge. They will resist this conclusion at every turn.

Space and purpose will not permit me to argue at length with self-avowed atheists or indifferent agnostics other than to say the following.

- The Old Testament (O.T.) records hundreds of prophecies, written many centuries before the coming of Jesus; yet they were precisely fulfilled in Him. This is reason enough to believe that the Bible is the Word of the Omniscient God: the One who knows the end from the beginning (Isa. 46.10).

- The New Testament (N.T.) is undergirded by a much greater number of centuries-old documents than any other piece of ancient writing. More than five thousand copies and fragments of the N.T., some dating back as far as the second and third centuries A.D., are still in existence. They are critical confirmations that 99.8 percent of our present N.T. is consistent with its autographs: the original writings of the N.T. authors. No variations within these extant writings alter anything pertaining to the central doctrines of the Christian faith.

- The historical fact that a man named Jesus Christ lived, died, and has been bodily raised from the dead is confirmed in the N.T. by many eyewitness accounts. That this man named Jesus was crucified nearly two thousand years ago finds little disputation among critics; but that He has been raised from the dead is yet another matter. Resurrection is the doctrine in dispute.

    Why is this so? Because in his or her own heart every person knows intuitively that to be convinced that Jesus Christ is risen from the dead compels solemn attention to the many other declarations made by and about Him in the Bible.

- The speculations of uninformed men about the question of what happens after we die promote nonsense. To be awakened to the truth, we must consult someone who has actually died, been buried, and has then been raised from the dead. That Someone is the subject of the historically reliable gospels that open up the N.T.

If anyone will submit to reading the gospels with a sincere and contrite heart, he will discover the truth. God has always been willing to reason with every person who will bow his knee with an ear to hear. He will make Himself known in a personal way to every such person.

The Bible contains news both bad and good, and I will present things in this order.

Sin and Law

The gospel of Jesus Christ includes the message of forgiveness of sin. And while the necessity of forgiveness may be frequently ignored in the ordinary affairs of human life, there are at least two occasions on which sin becomes an issue of considerable importance in the heart of every natural-born man.[1]

1. When one is sinned against, sin becomes a paramount vexation to that person. Even criminals are highly excited by transgressions against themselves.

2. When one is involved in some secret sin, he or she will devote every effort to conceal whatever that sin may be.

We are all out of the seed of our original progenitor, Adam. He and his wife became sinners,[2] and we have all inherited their sinful nature. For this reason every natural-born person has grown up to become—in

---

[1] My frequent use of the term "natural-born man" is with reference to everyone born (only) of the flesh: by the means of nature. Jesus says that we must be "born again," spiritually (John. 3.3ff). Have you been born again, dear reader?

[2] Chapter three of Genesis introduces the first sin of man.

varying degrees—proud, self-interested, self-reliant, self-indulgent, and self-righteous, holding fast to a personal sense of autonomy. In most cases men have very little use for God. He is rarely in the thoughts of the naturally-born: those begotten as kind after their own kind.[3]

This testimony of life and Scripture finds men thankless, crediting God with little or nothing in the ordinary days of their lives. Yet in times of calamity some of these same ones will call out to God—One unknown to them—in desperation. From indifference to desperate appeals—how contradictory is the nature of man before his Creator.

But this condition of mankind is not the entirely of his predicament. The prophet Jeremiah asks, "Can the Ethiopian change his skin, or the leopard his spots?" (Jer. 13.23). Suffering Job wondered, "How then can a man be righteous before God? Or how can he be clean who is born of a woman?" (Job 25.4). Isaiah simply declares, "The whole head is sick!" (Isa. 1.5). Though one's behavior may be modified by degree through self-determination, his human nature will remain unchanged; its unchangeableness is the consequence of sin.

We are informed by God's Word that sin is more than just an outward transgression. Sin is something that dwells within us (Rom. 7.20). The evidence of this fact is plain to see. No parent has ever had to spend any time teaching his toddler to do the wrong thing; for every child will evidence early on that a sin-nature dwells within him or her.

Sin is defined in the Bible as "the transgression of law" (1 John 3.4). Whether in thought or in deed, the presence and power of sin is revealed through law. The apostle Paul says, "Where there is no law there is no transgression."[4] But whenever a law (a rule or commandment) invades one's conscience, the sin that is already dwelling within him comes to life and may manifest itself in action.

---

[3] In the opening chapters of Genesis, the Bible establishes the principle of kind after its own kind: fish from fish, birds from birds, and sinners from sinners.

[4] Rom. 4.15; 7.9; 1 Cor. 15.56b.

Perhaps an illustration from ordinary life will be helpful here.

> A certain man may delight to drive 105 mph down the freeway in a state that has no speed limit. He is, therefore, no transgressor of law.
>
> However, if a 55 mph speed limit is one day enacted as law, suddenly his sinful nature springs to life and exposes itself for what it is. Our man does not like this new regulation. In fact, he hates it. It opposes his personal pleasure and his preference to do as he pleases.
>
> So, he buys a radar detector to help him disobey this statute. Only when his radar detector begins to squeal will fear bring him into instant compliance. On all other occasions he may likely, knowingly disobey this new law.

Sin operates along these same lines in adultery, extortion, deceit, thievery, etc. By nature, a man frequently opposes what is right, preferring what is wrong. He will excuse himself on the one hand; but on the other hand, like our speeder, he will do everything imaginable to keep from being caught in his transgression. What a conflict this is.

Law is an ordinance with a penalty attached for its violation. Different countries have different laws—ignorance of the law being no excuse. God has a moral Law, and ignorance of it is also without excuse. This is so because His Law is at work in the human heart through conscience. All men have been given to know right from wrong, their conscience either excusing or accusing them (Rom. 2.15).[5]

Man's problem is that he is out of sync with God, our Judge, as to how He feels about sin. A man may not participate in the grosser sins of life, thinking that by avoiding them he will be acquitted on the day of God's judgment. However, among the (so called) lesser sins that

---

[5] Concerning "the work of the law *[that universally implanted sense of right and wrong]* written in [our] hearts" (Rom. 2.15), Weymouth's N.T. reads, "a knowledge of the conduct which the Law requires is engraven on [our] hearts."

God abhors and will judge are these: pride of heart (observable in a proud look), mental adultery (lust), deceit, wicked thoughts and plans, evil desires, gossiping, boastfulness, hatred, contentiousness, jealousies, outbursts of anger, selfish ambitions, strife, envy, covetousness, hypocrisy, etc.[6] There will be no immunity granted by a holy God in His final prosecution of these matters.

We discover in Scripture that the Lord will not merely judge the outward behavior of men; for He "searches all hearts and understands all the intent of the thoughts *[therein]*" (1 Chron. 28.9). God is "a discerner of the thoughts and intents of the heart; and there is no creature hidden from His sight; but all things are naked and open to the eyes of Him to whom we must give account" (Heb. 4.12f).

God will ultimately reckon with men; but "because the sentence against an evil work is not executed speedily, therefore the heart of the sons of men is fully set in them to do evil" (Eccl. 8.11). Despite this delay, our benevolent God sometimes allows the cloak of a man's sin to be suddenly lifted, bringing sin and its consequences into present and shameful evidence. This allowance is intended to turn a man from darkness to Light in order that he may seek salvation and the forgiveness of sins in Christ before his future and final day of judgment.

Concerning that future day, I pause to take notice of the following misconception. Many people—including myself before I became a Christian—imagine that God's judgment will be according to His weighing one's (presumed) good thoughts and deeds against one's bad thoughts and deeds. Men's anxious though misguided anticipation is that the good will outweigh the bad, and that they will thereby be saved from condemnation. Yet this ungodly principle is not even according to the laws of society. The most right-living person in town, if he is convicted of murder or extortion, will not be saved from the law's just punishment. Even if he has done ten thousand good deeds, "Guilty as charged!" will be the verdict.

---

[6]   Prov. 6.17-19; Matt. 5.28; 7.21f; Rom. 1.29ff; 15.9,26; 16.5; Gal. 5.20,21.

In his remarks in chapter one of his epistle to the Romans, the apostle Paul describes a litany of the (even dreadful) conditions into which a man may descend, concluding that "although [men] know God's righteous decree—that those who do such things deserve death—they not only continue to do these very things but they also approve of those who practice them" (Rom. 1.32).

One's closest companions are frequently of a like mind with him respecting (bad) character and behavior; but in Num. 32.23 we are assured that every man's sin will ultimately find him out. While the totality of his sin and unrighteousness is impossible for any man to recall, the Omniscient One maintains an unfadable record (Heb 4.13).

Some may wonder: "Just how exacting are the requirements of God's moral Law?" The apostle James puts forth the following principle: "Whoever shall keep the whole Law, and yet stumble in one point, he has become guilty of all" (Jas. 2.10). Worse yet, God's Law is far stricter than most men think it to be: "Now if a person sins and does anything that the LORD has commanded not to be done, *even* though he was unaware, still he is guilty and shall bear his punishment" (Lev. 5.17).

It seems unnecessary to provide any lengthy explanations or examples in order to affirm the following three truths.

1. A person's unbelief and sin do not only bear upon his own personal, eternal destiny; they will also have a direct or an indirect effect upon the destiny of others, and will likely be imitated by his offspring. Even sin that is out of sight—sin that one may think is private and unknown—will, in some way, work its way out to endangering the future of his children.

2. Sin's activity within a natural-born person is so habitual that it is like breathing; it is so much a part of life that it generally goes without notice.

3. Every man's sin is ultimately against God and His Law.[7]
   If this is not so, why will God judge him?

Finally, regarding sin and law: Scripture affirms that God did not intend for His Law to set any person right with Him by his or her keeping the Ten Commandments. The purpose of God's Law is to reveal sin in every person (Rom. 3.20b). Until people come to understand that they are sinners, even becoming sick of their sin and having a heartfelt longing to be other than what they actually are, none are truly prepared to receive the good news contained in the gospel of Jesus Christ (see Job. 42.5).

The Fear of the Lord

"God is love" (1 John 4.8,16); this is one of the undeniable affirmations of Scripture concerning His character. Both these sweet words and the declaration in John 3.16 can be quickly recited from memory by many: even by those who have not come to a living faith in Christ. However, some may not know or may simply ignore something else that is three times recorded in the Bible—"God is a consuming fire."[8]

For half of my life I was an unbeliever and a wanton sinner. I can testify that I was frequently burdened by life's worries, often feeling hopeless. By midlife I had begun to fear what my end might be if I died in my many sins. What is your circumstance, dear reader?

Whatever is your case, be assured that when the fear of the Lord concerning sin comes upon any of us it is the evidence of God's intention to enlighten us; for the Bible informs us that the fear of the Lord is the beginning of knowledge and wisdom.[9]

---

[7] The narrative of King David's adulterous relationship with Bathsheba is recorded in Second Samuel, chap. 11. When the king learned that he had impregnated Bathsheba, he undertook a murderous scheme in an attempt to cover up his sin. When he later came to his right mind, David cried out, "Against You, You only, have I sinned and done that which is evil in Your sight" (Psa. 51.4).

[8] Deut. 4.24; 9.3; Heb. 12.29.

[9] Job 28.28; Psa. 111.10; Prov. 1.7; 9.10.

Consider an example from ordinary life concerning fear.

> Following a routine physical examination a man may be informed by his physician: "You have cancer, but more testing will confirm how advanced it is."
>
> The patient may respond in one of two extremes. If he is a fearless, self-assured but unwise man he may ignore his physician's warning and refuse further testing, declaring, "I feel fine; this cannot be my case." He therefore consigns himself to go off and to die of his affliction, denying himself of any possible cure.
>
> On the contrary, if he trusts the judgment of his physician and is in fear of dying (perhaps in spiritual unpreparedness), as a wise man he will undergo further tests and, if they prove positive for cancer, he will anxiously inquire, "Doctor! what must I do to be cured?"
>
> As it is in the natural, so it is in the spiritual. Our Creator and Great Physician has rendered His final diagnosis—the natural-born man is mortally infected with a sinful nature. Therefore, the wise man will cry out, "O God! what must I do to be saved?"

If there is any reader who has not yet truly known the fear of the Lord, I pray that he or she may soon become imbued with it through the wondrous workings of God's grace. The lyrics of *Amazing Grace*—perhaps the most famous Christian hymn ever written—say it well: "'Twas Grace that taught my heart to fear; and Grace, my fears relieved. How precious did that Grace appear the hour I first believed."[10]

Fear is according to God's grace and it is intended to stir a man up in the midst of his waywardness to recognize his danger. However, it is

---

[10] This hymn was written by John Newton in 1779. Being a slave trader, Newton was, by his own confession, a wicked and extravagant sinner before his conversion.

"the riches of [God's] kindness and forbearance and patience" that may ultimately lead any person to repentance (Rom. 2.4).

For how long has God been kind, forbearing and patient with you, dear reader? Oh, how great is the grace of God.

The Person of Christ

The N.T. opens wide a wonder that was typified though shrouded in the O.T.: the person of Jesus Christ. Jesus identified Himself and is declared throughout the N.T. to be the Son of God. Knowing this, His enemies accused Him of blasphemy; they reviled Him for making Himself equal with God.[11] Jesus nowhere refutes this accusation; for He who was with God in the beginning was God, and was the same One who became flesh, coming in the likeness of men to dwell among them.[12]

Jesus Christ is the very image of God's personage, all the fullness of the Godhead dwelling in Him bodily.[13] His words and His working of miracles were an open display of this truth. Nevertheless, one of Jesus' own disciples petitioned Him: "Lord, show us the Father, and it is enough for us." To this request Jesus unabashedly replied, "Have I been with you so long, and yet you have not known Me, Philip? He who has seen Me has seen the Father" (John; 14.8f). Matthew's gospel identifies Jesus Christ as "Immanuel...God with us" (Matt. 1.23).

Jesus' enemies set out to kill Him for His alleged blasphemy. Despite their accomplishment, He arose bodily from the dead the third day and appeared to certain disciples—not including Thomas. He later appeared to the unbelieving Thomas; and upon beholding the resurrected One, Thomas declared, "My Lord and my God!" Without reproving Thomas' profession, Jesus replied, "Because you have seen

---

[11] John 5.18; 10.33; 19.7. Jesus and the Father are one, in Spirit and by nature: ref. John 10.30,38.

[12] John 1.1,14; Phil. 2.7.

[13] Col. 1.15a; 2.9; Heb. 1.3.

Me, you have believed. Blessed are those who have not seen and have yet believed."[14]

Years later the apostle Paul wrote that the resurrected Christ "appeared to more than five hundred brethren at one time" (1 Cor. 15.6). Because of the uncompromising confession of those eyewitnesses, many suffered martyrdom for their testimony that Jesus arose from the dead and is Lord of all men.

Knowing this resurrected Christ by faith, and not merely knowing some things about Him, will enable us to see God as He truly is: full of grace and mercy in this day, His righteous wrath being reserved for a future day. "Now is the day of salvation" (2 Cor. 6.2).

Forgiveness

It is sin that separates men from God (Isa. 59.2). To be reconciled to God a person needs His forgiveness. But one may insist: "There in no way God can forgive my sins; they are too many and too great."

Really! The apostle Paul—known as Saul in his earlier life—confessed that he was formerly a luster and blasphemer, a violent persecutor of Christians, even consenting to their death.[15] Who is worse than Saul?

The wonderful good news is that God has provided a way unto forgiveness of any and all sin.[16] This is at the heart of the gospel of Christ.

Let us reason a little further on this subject of forgiveness; for the Word of God can always enlighten us (Psa. 18.28).

---

[14] John 20.19,20,26-29.

[15] Rom. 7.7f; Act. 8.1; 1 Tim. 1.13.

[16] There is only one exception to this truth. Jesus' enemies blasphemed the Holy Spirit when they claimed that He was possessed of the devil and cast out demons by the power of Satan. This one sin finds no forgiveness, neither in this age nor in the age to come; and such a blasphemer is in danger of eternal condemnation (Matt. 12.24,31,32; Mark 3.22,28-30).

Forgiveness is costly; it always costs somebody something. True forgiveness may be defined as "the willingness of one to absorb, into himself, the consequence (or loss) brought upon him by the transgression of another without requiring any recompense on the part of the transgressor."

Consider the following ordinary examples of this kind of forgiveness in the natural realm.

> Smith steals a chicken from Jones' barnyard for dinner. Immediately after killing it, he is remorseful, and he goes to Jones, retuning his property and asking for his forgiveness. Jones forgives Smith and requires no compensation from him, willingly suffering the loss—a dead chicken.

> Brown has incurred a debt of $10,000, but he is penniless. A benefactor may pay the debt without demanding any repayment. If Brown's benefactor is a multimillionaire, his benevolence has cost him little. On the other hand, if she is his aged mother, it may have cost her all of her living.

In the opening verses of Mark's gospel, chapter two, Jesus said to a paralytic man He had never met, "Child, your sins are forgiven." The enemies of Jesus who were in attendance reasoned that He was blaspheming, thinking, "Who can forgive sins but God alone?" Knowing their thoughts, Jesus replied, "Why are you reasoning about these things in your hearts? Which is easier—to say to the paralytic, 'Your sins are forgiven,' or to say, 'Get up, and pick up your bed and walk?'" (Think about this, dear reader. Which saying entails the lesser risk?) "'But in order that you may know that the Son of Man has authority on earth to forgive sins,' He said to the paralytic, 'I say to you, get up, pick up your bed and go home.'" Upon Jesus' command, the paralytic was immediately healed, picked up his bed and left the scene. (I am certain that the paralytic's blessing was more than physical.)

This is only one example of Jesus forgiving the sins of strangers; but it raises several questions.

1. How is God found righteous in forgiving sinners?

2. When did God, according to the definition of forgiveness above, willingly suffer the consequence of our sins unto Himself?

3. How much did it cost Him?

The answer is this: God suffered in Christ,[17] and forgiveness cost Him everything in the horrific and bloody torture of His body and the excruciating torment of His soul while dying on the cross.

Who Is Like Unto This God?

Since the beginning of this age men have honored and feared an incalculable number of gods. In their efforts to appease those gods they have offered up innumerable sacrifices, even unto the fiery sacrifice of their own children.[18] Imagine such a thing.

But the Bible declares that the LORD God is the God of gods (Deut. 10.17). What sacrifice does He require to fully appease His righteous wrath? None that a poor sinner can offer aside from what King David affirms in Psa. 51.17: "The sacrifices of God are a broken spirit; a broken and a contrite heart, O God, You will not despise."

Many men's ordinary conceptions of God may include some small imagination of His majesty in glory and His great and fearsome power. But will they ever consider His holiness, because of which sinful men are separated from Him? Will they ever be found in fear and trembling because of His wrath, one day to be unleashed?

But, dear reader, wonder at this: God—who is the Creator of all things seen and unseen—intended from eternity past to come among

---

[17] "God was in Christ" (Col. 1.19).

[18] Lev. 18.21; Deut. 12.31; Psa. 106.37.

men in the end of the ages, as a man, to willingly submit Himself to their mockings, scourging, and His own crucifixion, bearing the sins of men in His sinless body on the cross as a sacrifice for their sins, so that they might be reconciled to Him.[19]

Who can take in a God like this—a God who has provided Himself a sacrifice, in Christ, for sinners? This truth is admittedly too marvelous to be fully comprehended by our natural minds.

The Great Exchange

As an ambassador for Christ, I implore you on His behalf, "Be reconciled to God." Paul assures men that they can be reconciled to God because "the One who knew no sin was made sin for us, in order that we might become the righteousness of God in [Christ]" (2 Cor. 5.20f). A great exchange indeed.

No man who hopes to be acquitted by God and to be reconciled to Him by doing good and avoiding evil will ever achieve his hoped-for end. Why? Because he does not and cannot keep all the moral Law of God unfalteringly. Furthermore, he lacks any means by which he may cancel his sin-debt to that Law. He remains, therefore, a law-breaker, a transgressor, a guilty sinner, and under a curse.[20] But the wondrous good news to all who will believe is this: "Christ has redeemed us from the curse of the Law, having become a curse for us."[21]

Saved by Grace through Faith

All natural-born men are living by some kind of faith: faith in money, power, or influence; faith in their good health, talents, or abilities; faith

---

[19] "Reconciled"—"made right with another": 2 Cor. 5.20f; 1 Pet. 2.24; Heb. 9.28.

[20] John 3.36b; Gal. 3.10.

[21] Gal. 3.10-13. Here, the word "redeemed" means "to exchange for money, goods or something else considered to be of value." God Himself redeemed His children; He took possession of them by paying the ransom price required under Law. The price was blood—in this case, it was the blood of Jesus. This is the incomparable redemption of the ages.

in the assumed fidelity of their spouse; faith in government; etc. And while they may feel some sense of assuredness in these and other like things as they face tomorrow, these frail objects of faith will one day (at least, in their last day) fail to be of any eternal value. But faith in God's faithfulness to His Word will prove to be everlasting.

The apostle Paul assures us "that a man is justified *[made right with God]* by faith apart from the deeds of law."[22] The Lawgiver has provided this superior provision for all men who are the subjects of condemnation under "the Law of sin and death" (Rom. 8.2). One may be acquitted by faith—faith in God's Word, which Word is Christ, the Word made flesh (John 1.14). Paul had said earlier, "Now a righteousness of God apart from law has been manifested, being witnessed by the Law and the prophets *[in the O.T.]*, even a righteousness of God through faith in Jesus Christ for all those who believe" (Rom. 3.21f).

"Christ is an end of law unto righteousness" (Rom. 10.4). Bless the Lord for this provision in and through His Son. On man's behalf, this end has been accomplished through Jesus' fulfilling all the righteous requirements of the Law (Matt. 5.17), even suffering its consequence.

Dear reader, hear with rejoicing what the Biblical writers say further. When Jesus suffered death in the stead of sinners who will believe in Him, they were "released from the Law" (Rom. 7.6)."[23] Christ "wiped out the handwriting of requirements that was against [all who believe]" (Col. 2.14). Though the Law was "weak through the flesh" (Rom. 8.3), the writer of Hebrews says, "there is a setting aside *[a cancelling, a putting away, an abolishing]* of a former commandment because of its weakness and uselessness; for the Law made nothing perfect" (Heb. 7.18f).

---

[22] Rom. 3.26b-28.

[23] To be "released from the Law" means that one who believes in Christ has been saved (released) from the eternal curse of the Law of sin and death. It does not mean that one is no longer under any Law; for God's moral Law has been continually in effect since the beginning, and it will remain in effect forever. It is only the Law's penalty that we are concerned about here.

Under a law of works we hear God declare this: "Keep My statutes and My judgments, by which a man may live if he does them."[24] The promise and provision brought in through Christ says: "He who believes in the Son has eternal life" (John 3.36a). These are two very different principles.

If I would know the truth about life, death, and the hereafter, I would be wise to listen to the words of one who has passed through life, into death, and out of it through resurrection (this being no kind of near death experience). Christ is that One. He is the wisdom of God, and God commands all men: "Hear [My Son]"…"in whom are hidden all the treasures of wisdom and knowledge."[25]

It is sad to say, but true: most men are unwise, trusting in their own opinions and in the opinions of others more than they trust in the sure Word of God.

Having reasoned with you from the Word of God, I pray that if you were uncertain earlier on, you may now be persuaded concerning the way of salvation out from under the fear of death and condemnation. Scripture assures all of us that whosoever will acknowledge his sinful separation from God; and will yet approach God in prayer, confessing his sin in brokenness, seeking God's mercy; and will believe in his heart that his sin is put away in the sacrifice of God's now risen Son; and if he is willing to confess before men that Jesus Christ is Lord…he shall be saved![26]

"What Shall We Do?"

This was the question asked by those who heard and believed the apostle Peter's first preaching nearly two thousand years ago. He had concluded his message by testifying that "God has raised up this Jesus,

---

[24] Lev. 18.5; Neh. 9.29c; Ezek. 20.11.

[25] Mark 9.7 followed by Col. 2.3.

[26] Prov. 28.13; John 3.14f; Rom. 10.9f; Heb. 9.26.

and of that we are all witnesses…Know for certain, therefore, that God has made Him both Lord and Christ—this Jesus whom you crucified" (Acts 2.32ff). His message convinced about three thousand people of their complicity in the crucifixion of their long awaited Messiah: the One whom they rejected when He first appeared.

Those who came under conviction upon hearing Peter's message were anxious in their inquiring, "What shall we do?"

To them Peter gave the answer, and his answer applies to this day. "Repent, and let every one of you be baptized in the name of Jesus Christ for the remission *[forgiveness]* of your sins; and you shall receive the gift of the Holy Spirit…Be saved from this perverse *[corrupt]* generation" (Acts 2.38ff).

Many of those who were convicted by Peter's message had doubtless been gathered, only weeks earlier, with the ones who had heard Pontius Pilate inquire aloud, "What shall I do with Jesus?" That mob cried out, "Crucify Him!…Crucify Him!" (Matt. 27.22f).

Some who heard Peter's message may likely have heard Jesus earlier calling out to them, "Come unto Me, all you who labor and are heavy-laden, and I will give you rest" (Matt. 11.28). His same calling is in effect today, dear reader. Are you heavy-laden with the worries and troubles of life, and the fear of death?

"It Is Finished!"

With His dying breaths Jesus cried out from the cross, "It is finished!" (John 19.30). When He expired, reconciliation with God was opened wide for every person who will call upon His Name in faith. The resurrection of Jesus Christ from the dead is God's proof positive that He is Lord of all (Acts 10.36); that Life comes through faith in this crucified/resurrected One (1 Pet. 1.3); and that He is the way unto salvation for every person who will truly believe in Him (Acts 4.12).

What an amazing salvation this is.

During His days of ministry Jesus said, "I have not come to call the righteous, but sinners to repentance."[27] In another place He gives assurance that He came "to give His life a ransom for many" (Matt. 20.28). Yet His unabashed declaration is, "No one comes to the Father except through Me" (John 14.6). Will you come to Him today, dear reader, in order that you may have forgiveness of sins and eternal life; or do you remain unwilling (cp. John 5.40)?

While he is alive, a man's estate is only one of two: "He who believes in the Son has eternal life; but he who does not believe the Son will not see life, but the wrath of God abides upon him" (John 3.36).[28] The present and future circumstance between him who believes and him who is doubtful or disinterested in salvation is indeed serious.

A prophet of old declared: "Multitudes, multitudes in the valley of decision! For the day of the LORD is near in the valley of decision" (Joel 3.14). "The day of the LORD" is the day of His vengeance.[29] If you are still in a spiritual "valley of decision," you remain in danger.

> John 8.24   *[Jesus says to the unbelieving]* "You shall die in your sins; for unless you believe that I am He *[God, in human flesh]*, you shall die in your sins."

Paul says that anyone who has heard of Jesus but has not come to Him in faith has judged himself unworthy of eternal life (cp. Acts 13.46); but if you are one who has truly come to Him in faith, you now have eternal life. Confess your faith, be baptized, and receive the gift of the Holy Spirit.[30]

"Who do you say that I am?" This is the question Jesus Christ has put before men. It is a question of life or death.

---

[27] Luke 5.32; Matt. 9.13b; Mark 2.17b.

[28] This verse appears in the same chapter with John 3.16: "For God so loved the world...."

[29] While this passage from Joel has reference to an actual, future day, it has spiritual application to every unbeliever's present circumstance in life.

[30] Mark 16.16; Rom. 10.9,10; Acts 2.38.

Chapter 2

An Introduction to Believers

There are believers young and old. If some of the old souls have difficulty with certain views put forth in chapters to follow, their perplexity may be the result of years of complacency in doctrinal assumptions that are not according to Christ. Such assumptions are cherished by men and are hard to be shaken off. I hope that every serious minded believer will search the Scriptures to confirm what is the truth in every matter (Acts 17.11). This is our individual responsibility.

Our coming to an intimate knowledge of Christ as our resurrection life, and not merely our superior knowledge of doctrine, is far more important than the number of years we have been Christians. In the end, correct doctrine must bring in the death of our old man and new life in Christ. This transition requires a renewing of our mind (Eph. 4.22ff).

Having been stoned and beaten with whips and rods on numerous occasions, in constant peril of both Jews and Gentiles, and having suffered hunger and thirst, cold and nakedness...nevertheless the apostle Paul's daily concern was not only for himself, but for all the churches.[1] I had often read about Paul's life since my earliest days as a believer; yet more than a dozen years rolled by before I found myself considering the following thoughts and questions.

---

[1] 2 Cor. 11.23-28; 2 Tim. 2.10.

1. Paul was originally an avowed enemy and persecutor of
    Christians, but he was saved one day through a miracu-
    lous encounter with the risen Lord Jesus (Acts 9). I
    wondered: "Why did Paul gladly and diligently submit
    himself to such a difficult and perilous life thereafter?"

2. I am a Christian; but my life finds no actual likeness to
    Paul's. Therefore, simply based on the fact that I had
    also been brought to faith in Jesus, I wondered further:
    "Will there be no distinctions made among believers in
    the end of things; and are there to be any consequences
    for Christians if we simply live a lackluster (or worse, a
    disobedient) life after being saved?"

3. "Is there something in God's plan of salvation that I
    have not yet discovered in my early years as a believer?"

Some months after these thoughts began to intrude upon my mind
and heart, my wife and I were enjoying dinner with a precious couple
in the Lord at the Yum Yum Tree in Honolulu. During a discussion of
my musings with my dear friend, David, he made the following comment: "We hold that eternal life is the gift of God apart from works (by
grace through faith alone); but that inheritance of the kingdom will be a
reward according to works." Though he continued talking, I was no
longer listening, having been caught off-guard by his remark. When my
attention returned to our conversation, I interrupted David to ask,
"What did you just say?" After I joggled his recollection, he recalled
and repeated what he had said moments earlier, word for word.

That one statement was instrumental in my beginning to search the
Scriptures and the works of numerous Bible commentators to see
whether it might be true. Even my early investigations brought me to a
new, unimagined understanding of God's objective in saving men. I
have since come to see a central theme that permeates the N.T.; that
theme is the kingdom of God and its inheritance.

This subject will be opened up later in this writing.

The N.T.'s message concerning salvation is so plain that a youngster is able to come to a true and living faith in Jesus Christ. Yet, it is also a deep and mysterious Book containing "some things hard to be understood" (2 Pet. 3.16). So much truth is distributed throughout the Bible that many remarkable and godly men—some having spent their entire adult lifetime studying it—have been forced to admit that there are a number of things recorded therein that have remained a mystery to them. In contrast to these saintly ones, there are some who have given themselves to much Biblical investigation, yet their personal lives do not reflect the things they have studied. This is most unfortunate; for Scripture makes it clear that truth manifested in godly character and conduct is God's desire for all who are His children.

Matthew's gospel presents these words of Jesus, spoken to His disciples: "Seek first the kingdom of God and His righteousness" (Matt. 6.33). Yet we are assured by the apostle Paul that every Christian has been "transferred into the kingdom of [God's] dear Son" (Col. 1.13f), having a present righteousness through faith in Christ (Phil 3.9). It would be very curious indeed if Christians are being called to seek things that are already theirs. There must, therefore, be some things other than Christ's righteousness and His present kingdom (things that are a part of our current, common salvation) that believers are to seek after. So the question becomes, "How may we reconcile the seeming inconsistency of seeking while yet having?"

I will consider this question and its answer in chapters to follow.

Over two thousand pages are devoted to the subject of the kingdom of God[2] in George N. H. Peters' three-volume work entitled *The Theocratic Kingdom* (Kregel Publications), and it is my task to summarize the great significance of the kingdom in this short writing.

---

[2]   While "the kingdom of God" is inclusive of "the kingdom of heaven," any further distinction in their meanings would contribute nothing to this writing. Notice, in fact, that the two terms often appear to be synonymous—cp. Matt. 19.23 with 19.24; Matt. 4.17 with Mark 1.15; Matt. 13.31 with Mark 4.30 and Luke 13.18f; Matt. 19.14 with Mark 10.14 and Luke 18.16.

Notwithstanding this difficulty, I will endeavor to confirm that the kingdom into which all believers are being called (1 Thess. 2.12) is a specific kingdom: one which a believer must be adjudged by Christ to be worthy of inheriting. This kingdom will be thoroughly discussed from Chapter 8 onward; for God's foremost message to the Church concerns this kingdom and its inheritance.

The world, as a whole, is completely unaware that even now "the LORD reigns."[3] Of old it has been declared, "The Most High is the ruler over the kingdom of mankind and bestows it on whomever He wishes"; "the Heavens do rule."[4] They rule to such a degree that world events and even the circumstances of our personal lives are influenced by them, while the Sovereign God of the universe oversees all things. God's present sovereignty is unimagined, unconsidered, and resisted by most of mankind in these evil days. There is, however, a day ahead when Jesus Christ will be manifested unto all of creation as the "Lord of lords and King of kings" (Rev. 17.14). It will be a time when "the kingdom of the world [will] become *the kingdom* of our Lord and of His Christ" (Rev. 11.15).

I wonder if you, dear reader, can recall any time you have ever heard a specific message concerning inheritance of this coming king-dom. The answer of many will likely be, "Never." This seems odd; for John the Baptist preached the nearness of this kingdom when he com-manded his audiences: "Repent! for the kingdom of the heavens is at hand" (Matt. 3.2). Jesus' ministry was inaugurated with exactly the same words (Matt. 4.17). Nearly two thousand years ago, while Jesus was ministering in the presence of His adversaries, He declared, "the king-dom of God has come upon you" (Luke 11.20). He said this because He (mankind's unrecognized King) was then dwelling among men.

---

[3]   Psa. 93; 96; 99.

[4]   2 Chron. 20.6f; Psa. 83.18; Jer. 27.5; Dan. 4.17,25c,26. Even unbelievers and the wicked unwittingly "do whatever [God's] hand and [His] plan foreor-dained to take place" (Acts 4.28)—consider Pharaoh's plight (Exo. 4.21).

Since Jesus' ascension unto the right hand of the Father the kingdom of God, unseen by the world, has continued until now in spiritual reality as the Holy Spirit ministers within and among believers worldwide. However, the manifest reality of His kingdom will finally come into open display for the whole world to see under the authority of the Man, Christ Jesus, when He returns to earth from His present place of abode. (There is a Man seated in the highest heaven at this very moment.)[5] The gospels, and the N.T. epistles (written by apostles of our Lord to believers), are filled with encouragements and warnings concerning the inheritance of this future kingdom.

Paul, on a return journey to Jerusalem, knowing that chains and afflictions awaited him there, unwaveringly declared to certain elders:

> Acts 20.24,25,27,31   None of these things move me; nor do I count my life dear to myself, so that I may finish my race with joy, and the ministry which I received from the Lord Jesus, to testify to the gospel of the grace of God. And indeed, now I know that you all, among whom I have gone preaching the kingdom of God, will see my face no more…I have not shunned to declare to you the whole counsel of God…for three years I did not cease to admonish each one with tears.

The "whole counsel of God" is not merely the message of Jesus as man's Savior. Will one suppose that Paul spent three years preaching the first things of the Gospel to the same (saved) people over and over again?[6] No. He taught them the whole counsel of God, which includes Christ's kingdom teachings. These teachings are intended to encourage and build up the saints to eagerly anticipate His future coming; for there is a day approaching when Christ will begin to visibly rule and reign over the world in righteousness with His joint-heirs (Rom. 8.17b).

There is "another King" (Acts 17.7), and He is coming. Although the full gospel message is rarely heard in our day—even in assemblies

---

[5] Acts 2.33; 7.55f; Rev. 5.6; 7.17.

[6] Acts 5.42; and see 1 Cor. 15.3f concerning things "of first importance" (NASB).

that denominate themselves as "full gospel"—Jesus has assured us that "this gospel of the kingdom will be preached in all the world as a witness to all the nations, and then the end will come" (Matt. 24.14).

May the Spirit and the Word help us all to clearly understand what is the high, heavenly calling of God in Christ Jesus, in order that we may be watching and ready, established in the hope of being glorified together with Him.

Beloved ones, it is to this end that we have been and are being called.[7]

---

[7]   1 Thess. 2.12; 2 Thess. 2.14; 1 Pet. 5.10.

Chapter 3

A Gift Versus A Reward

Scripture makes a distinction between the "gift" of eternal life (Rom. 6.23) and the "reward" of the inheritance (Col. 3.24). Therefore, it is important that we examine the definitional difference between these two words, since they are not synonymous in any language. Understanding their separate meanings will be important as we continue on.

A Gift

Men do not identify a gift with something earned; in ordinary language we do not equate gifting with entitlement. The disposition and grace of the giver is the only determinant factor in one's giving a gift to another. Likewise, the gift of God's salvation from condemnation is not based upon merit. If it was, no man would be found worthy of such a thing. God's gift cannot be earned; it is free—but one does have to receive it.

Eternal life is God's gracious gift, not according to works. This gift includes the forgiveness of sins; it is irrevocable and the present possession of all who have been saved by grace through faith in the Lord Jesus Christ; it also includes the promise of resurrection. Only the following few verses from the N.T. should suffice to confirm these fundamental and glorious truths.

John 3.36a   Whosoever believes in the Son has eternal life

John 6.39   This is the will of the Father who sent Me, that of all He has given Me I should lose nothing, but I should raise it up in the last day.

Rom. 6.23   For the wages of sin is death, but the gift of God is eternal life in Jesus Christ our Lord.

Rom. 11.29   The gifts and calling of God are without repentance [i.e., they are irrevocable].

Eph. 1.7a   In [Christ] we have redemption through His blood, the forgiveness of our sins [cp. 1 John 2.12]

Eph. 2.8,9   For by grace you have been saved through faith, and that not of yourselves; it is the gift of God, not of works, lest anyone should boast.

These verses should be of great assurance to every Christians. Let all who are trusting in Jesus be of the same mind with the apostle Paul who was "persuaded that neither death nor life, nor angels nor principalities nor powers, nor things present nor things to come, nor height nor depth, nor any other created thing, shall be able to separate us from the love of God which is in Christ Jesus our Lord" (Rom. 8.38f).

Lamentably, there are those who hold that one can lose his salvation: their reference being to the gift of eternal life. This assumption is causing unnecessary strife and uncertainty among and within many who have been born again. The gift of eternal life cannot be lost. However, there is something to be gained or lost by believers, as we shall discover. However, that something does not pertain to everlasting life in the numberless ages of eternity.

A Reward

A reward (or, a prize)[1] is not according to grace alone; it is something merited, something of which one must be deemed worthy to receive.

---

[1]   In the N.T. Greek texts the words *antapódosin* (rendered as "reward" in Col. 3.24), *misthos* ("wage," "reward," or "hire") and *brabeion* ("prize") are always in the singular number. I am fully persuaded that these words refer to one and the same thing. More on this as we continue.

Hear what the apostle Paul has to say to us.

> 1 Cor. 9.24-27   Do you not know that those who are running in a race all run, but one receives the prize? Run in such a way that you may obtain it. 25 And everyone who is competing *for a prize* is temperate in all things. Now they *[in the natural realm compete]* to obtain a perishable crown, but we *[who run in the spiritual realm, aspire to obtain]* an imperishable *crown.* 26 Therefore I run thus: not with uncertainty. Thus I fight: not as one who beats the air. 27 But I discipline my body and bring it into subjection, lest, when I have preached to others, I myself should become disqualified.

Here, Paul is urging all believers to run in such a way that they might obtain the prize. But his admonition implies that the opposite could prove to be the case: viz., of not winning it through becoming disqualified. Paul said that he was living resolutely, vigorously, and temperately, and he preached the same to others. The reason? In order that none of us should be found disqualified of receiving an imperishable crown from the hand of the Lord at the end of our individual race of faith (cp. 2 Tim. 4.8). In this place, Paul is not taking any notice of the irrevocable gift of eternal life which he, like every person begotten of God, had already obtained by grace through faith in Christ.

Reward According to Works

The reward of Christ is obtained through being adjudged as worthy to receive it. "According to works" is the overarching principle of God's righteous judgment and recompense in the case of every man.[2] No Christian was ever saved from his (otherwise) just deserts by good works; yet he will be judged in the end according to his work of faith since becoming a Christian. Every believer was saved in order that he may do good works following upon his salvation (Eph. 2.10).

---

[2] "According to works" (Matt. 16.27) in the case of every Jew, Gentile, and Christian. See also Job 34.11; Psa. 62.12; Prov. 24.12; Rom. 2.6; Rev. 2.23.

This is not to imply that the grace of God has no part in the good deeds of believers. To the contrary: no believer's works are esteemed as worthy by God outside of the Holy Spirit's working them within him. No man, including a Christian, will make his boast before God in works done in the flesh—at the inclinations of his natural disposition. Furthermore, such works frequently result in mischief. In his writings to believers in Philippi and Colossae, Paul deals with the necessity of our working through God's working in us.

> Phil. 2.12,13   Therefore, my beloved, as you have always obeyed, not as in my presence only, but now much more in my absence, work out your own salvation with fear and trembling; 13 for it is God who works in you both to will and to do for His good pleasure.

> Col. 1.28,29 We proclaim [Christ], admonishing every man and teaching every man with all wisdom, so that we may present every man perfect [*mature*] in Christ. 29 For this purpose also I labor, striving according to His power, which works mightily within me.

While it is God's working in us that produces what is acceptable to Him, Scripture elsewhere tells us that our doing of righteous deeds is not divorced from our responsibility. John the Revelator writes: "His wife has made herself ready; and it was given to her to clothe herself in fine linen, bright and clean; for the fine linen is the righteous deeds of the saints" (Rev. 19.7f). John the Baptist commanded, "Bring forth fruit worthy of repentance" (Matt. 3.8): i.e., we are to bring forth fruit.

Reward is granted according to worthiness. This principle is affirmed by both Jesus and Paul. "The laborer is worthy of his wage."[3]

In another place, Paul makes a clear distinction between God's gift and His reward when he says, "Now to him who works, his wage [*or, reward*] is not reckoned according to grace, but as a debt" (Rom. 4.4).

---

[3] "...his wage"(Greek, *misthos*): i.e., "his hire," "his reward." See Luke 10.7; 1 Tim. 5.18; and cp. Lev. 19.13.

Now it is surely true that God is not indebted—in our usual understanding of this word—to do anything other than what He pleases. Nevertheless, it has pleased Him to put Himself under this obligation by His own Word; for God has identified Himself as "a Rewarder of those who diligently seek Him" (Heb. 11.6).

It should be clear that we Christians will not be rewarded simply because we have been saved by grace through faith. Worthiness of reward will be the issue of Christ's judgment when He examines our work of faith. He will know whether our works were done under the unction of the Holy Spirit. But how many believers are frequently or nearly always quenching this Spirit of grace indwelling them?

God's grace being freely given, one must nevertheless employ its means and opportunities.

Three principal conclusions on the subject of works are these.

1. No work is sufficient to reconcile[4] anyone to God.

2. Nevertheless, there are good works—works which God has ordained for those reconciled to Him—in which believers are called to walk.

3. The immutable principle of God's ultimate, righteous judgment, whether good or bad, will be "to every man according to his works."

I will have more to say on this last point in later chapters.

In closing out this section I would add this little bit. When Paul says he is "pressing on toward the mark for the prize of the high calling of God in Christ Jesus" (Phil. 3.14), he is not saying that he is pressing on to receive what he is already in possession of: eternal life.

The reward is an inheritance with Christ in His kingdom, as we shall see.

---

[4] Here, "to reconcile" is "to put away the estrangement or the enmity that exists between God and a man, woman or a young person."

The Consequences of Indifference

Having discussed the subject of works-based reward with many believers over the years, some have replied: "Well, I'm not concerned about rewards; I'm just grateful that I'm saved."

In all candidness I must admit that I myself was of a similar persuasion some two decades ago. But I have come to see that to hold and to express such disinterest is actually to despise one's birthright; for we are being called to attain unto the reward of the inheritance by our Rewarder. If it has pleased God to encourage us unto righteous thinking and righteous living by placing a reward before our spiritual eyes, who is the wise man who will ignore the opportunity of obtaining it?

Many teachers and preachers only make a distinction between receiving or not receiving our reward before the judgment seat of Christ. In so doing they ignore Paul's mention of the bad that may be awaiting some thereat—see 2 Cor. 5.10, which verse we will later consider at length. Though all who have been saved will one day enter experientially into eternal life, those found unworthy before His judgment seat may receive things worse than their loss of reward.

Consider three principles from ordinary life that Paul presented as divine, doctrinal illustrations to his disciple, Timothy; and may the Lord grant us a right understanding of these things.

> 2 Tim. 2.3-6   You must therefore endure hardship as a good soldier of Jesus Christ. 4 No man warring as a soldier entangles himself with the affairs of this life, in order that he may please him who enlisted him as a soldier. 5 And also, if anyone competes in athletics, he is not crowned unless he competes according to the rules. 6 The hardworking farmer must be first *[before others]* to partake of the crops.

Concerning Paul's last mention (v. 6): while the slothful farmer will surely fail of a fruitful crop, he will likely suffer more consequences than this. His slothfulness may find him without any money to pay his debts, or even to buy food or medicine for his family; they may become homeless, hungry, and sickly. Under this same principle, some Christian's may be discovered at the judgment seat to be not only fruitless, but impoverished; such ones will therefore experience the consequences of their slothfulness.

An Ignoble End

> 1 Cor. 3.10-15   According to the grace of God which was given to me, as a wise master builder I have laid the foundation, and another builds on it. But let each one take heed how he builds on it.
>
> 11 For no other foundation can anyone lay than that which is laid, which is Jesus Christ. 12 Now if anyone builds on this foundation *with* gold, silver, *or* precious stones, *[versus]* wood, hay, *or* stubble, 13 each one's work will become clear; for the Day will declare it, because it will be revealed by fire; and the fire will test each one's work, as to what sort it is.
>
> 14 If anyone's work which he has built on endures, he will receive a reward. 15 If anyone's work is burned, he will suffer loss; but he himself will be saved, yet so as through fire.

Even in this warning passage Paul upholds a doctrine of eternal security (v. 15).[5] Nevertheless, he testifies that some may experience an ignoble and hurtful end when their work is tried by fire on that Day.

Wood, hay, and stubble are easily gathered to build a hut, even upon a solid foundation. However, the mining of gold, silver, and precious stones to use in the construction of a glorious abode requires great effort on the part of any person who will so labor. Common metal anodized to appear as precious will be revealed by fire to be what it truly is; likewise, the true worth of a man's works will be revealed.

Paul warns us: "Let him who thinks he stands *[under the New Covenant]* take heed lest he should fall" (1 Cor. 10.12).

---

[5]   I will deal with the specific issue of salvation's security in our next chapter.

Summary

Understanding the difference between a "gift" and a "reward" is important for three reasons.

1. To allow us to know that God's Word makes a clear distinction between them

2. To establish the fact that Scripture discloses that this distinction is founded upon differing principles: the gift of eternal life is granted upon faith alone, while reward is based upon our work of faith after having been saved

3. To assure the believer that it is not the wicked and unbelieving only who will come into judgment before the Lord

Paul writes to Christians—immediately after referring to the judgment seat of Christ in 2 Cor. 5.10—"Therefore, *[personally]* knowing the fear of the Lord, we persuade men *[concerning judgment]*" (v. 11).

Beloved, be not deceived! "For he who does wrong will receive the consequences of the wrong which he has done, and there is no respect of persons" (Col. 3.25). Christ will be the righteous Judge.

A man of the world who walks after the flesh and takes advantage of every opportunity in this life may one day obtain the benefits of earthly comfort and economic security above his peers. This principle in natural life is plainly observable. And as it is in the natural realm, so it is in the spiritual realm. Paul gives recognition to this truth when he both warns and encourages believers: "For he who sows to his flesh will of the flesh reap corruption; but he who sows to the Spirit will, of the Spirit, reap everlasting life. So let us not grow weary in well-doing, for in due season we shall reap if we do not lose heart" (Gal. 6.8f).

Let us press on, dear Christian, to obtain the prize—the reward of the inheritance—which is set before us.

Chapter 4

Salvation's Security

With respect to something mentioned in our previous chapter, I will now specifically comment on an opinion commonly held by many Christians who say that one can lose his salvation: their reference being to the gift of eternal life. I cannot embrace this notion, and I contend that holding to such an assumption may cause a believer to stumble as he tries to move along in faith. May it never be that God—who has warranted the promise of eternal life by sealing it in the blood of Jesus—should ever fail of this promise.

If being born of God is a gift (and it is); and if the gifts of God are irrevocable (and they are); and if regeneration brings in eternal life (and it does); then the only remaining question seems to be, "Is one truly born of God able to be unborn at some future point in time for any reason, on his part or on God's?" Such a possibility is as impossible in the spiritual as it is in the natural.

Being born of God is not brought about by (simple) intellectual concurrence with Biblical propositions. Rather, being begotten of Him is a supernatural transaction. It brings in a new relationship with God; we become His children (Rom. 8.15ff).

While a worthless son may be disinherited by his father, this will in no way annul the fact that he is flesh of his father's flesh and life of his father's life. A simple DNA test will confirm what is true. Likewise, the spiritual DNA of a child of God is unalterable; he is what he is (God's child) and he has what he has (God's eternal life) by the grace of God.

However, as is the case among men, a child of God may turn out to be a disgrace to his Father's name. The Father may consequently revoke a certain inheritance that His child could have otherwise come into. Hear what Paul has to say concerning the range of possibilities that pertain to the life of God's begotten ones.

> 2 Tim. 2.11-13   For if we died with [Christ], we shall also live with Him. 12 If we endure, we shall also reign together with Him. If we deny Him, He also will deny us. 13 If we are faithless, He remains faithful; for He cannot deny Himself.

Here we read that He (Christ) will deny us if we deny Him; yet He will remain faithful to His Word, for He cannot deny Himself. What does His denial have to do with? It has only to do with denying those mute believers, and the ones who will not endure the trials of faith, and those who simply turn back, the privilege of reigning with Him in His kingdom. The author of Hebrews writes: "'If [a believer] draws back,' God says, 'My soul has no pleasure in him'" (Heb. 10.38). The gift of eternal life is not the subject of verse 12, above. In that verse, Christ's denial has reference only to a salvation which is to be revealed in glory in His kingdom reign. This will all become clear in chapters to follow.

Let us notice a few examples from the N.T. of believers who fell by the wayside during their Christian journey.

- There was Demas. He was once a fellow laborer with Paul; but Demas later forsook him, "having loved this present world [age]" (2 Tim. 4.10).

- There is the case of Hymenaeus and Alexander, whom Paul "handed over to Satan so that they might learn not to blaspheme" (1 Tim. 1.20).

- The saints in Corinth among whom an incestuous fellow was abiding were commanded by Paul to "deliver such a one to Satan for the destruction of the flesh, in order that his spirit may be saved in the day of the Lord" (1 Cor. 5.1ff).[1]

- Certain believers in Corinth were chastened of the Lord unto weakness, sickliness and even unto death for unworthily partaking of the Lord's Table. These things came to pass in order that these believers "should not be condemned with the world" (1 Cor. 11.26ff).

- Ananias and Sapphira—being believers in the church in Jerusalem but having lied to the Holy Spirit in a certain matter—each fell down dead at the feet of the apostle Peter (Acts 5.1ff).

These are examples of wayward Christians who suffered temporal judgments by both men and God; but nothing is said or implied about their losing the gift of God's eternal life.

In reply to the view of those who hold that eternal life, once owned upon faith, may be lost for some (or any) reason, I say, "Never!" That there are believers who may suffer things even greater than natural death is undeniably a possibility (Heb. 10.28f). But none of those who belong to Christ, who have been begotten of God, whose names are recorded in the Book of Life, shall ever be eternally cast away into the Lake of Fire (hell).[2] Eternal life, experientially, is God's promised end for all true Christians (Rom. 6.23); and "the Lord knows those who are His" (2 Tim 2.19).

---

[1] The incestuous one noted in 1 Cor. 5.5 was surely a believer—"that his spirit may be saved in the day of the Lord." See his outcome in 2 Cor. 2.6ff.

   With respect to those turned over to Satan, let us wonder: "How will one turn over to Satan someone who is already his?" This deliverance unto Satan was clearly intended as remedial and not punitive in both 1 Cor. 5.5 and 1 Tim. 1.20. Such deliverances unto Satan are disciplinary, in anticipation of their proving to be effectual chastenings in a Christian's life. See Heb. 12.8ff concerning the fact of and the reason for God's chastenings of His own.

[2] John 6.37,39; Rev. 20.15.

Confusion over this matter of salvation's security has entrapped millions of Christians in one of two difficulties.

1. Some, being in fear as to whether they may still be saved when they stumble into gross sin, become hamstrung in their attempt to move on in the confidence of God's mercy, grace, and unfailing love. They may even now repent and cry out, "Have mercy on me, O LORD, for I am in trouble!" (Psa. 31.9). He will hear.

2. Others lack a true fear of the Lord, the lack of which has led them into deceit. They may think that their soul's wellbeing before God is always alright, no matter what—"For" they may boast "I am under the Blood."

Teaching the insecurity of eternal salvation denigrates the gospel. However, no one who calls himself a Christian should take any careless, presumptuous comfort in the irrevocable gift of God; for there is to be a day of reckoning with all of His own.

One last wonderful truth concerning salvation, and then we will move on. All of the ransomed are out from under the ownership of a former master who kept us in bondage to sin and the fear of death. But our new Owner has given us assurance through the words of His Son: "All that the Father gives Me will come to Me, and the one who comes to Me I will by no means cast out" (John 6.37).

Nevertheless, some of God's children may have wandered off as lost sheep (Luke 15.4ff) since having been begotten of Him. How are you doing, beloved?

Chapter 5

Justification—Its Two Aspects

"Justification" and "righteousness" derive from the same Greek word, *dikaios*. In the N.T., to be righteous or justified means "being deemed upright in an ethical sense" and/or "being free of guilt under law." All Christians have been set free from the penalty of the Law of sin and death (Rom. 8.2). However, the former half of this definition pertains to what will be made known in a future day when Christ has examined our heart's condition and our work of faith.

By Faith

Justification by faith is a tenet of Christian orthodoxy and held by all true believers.

Paul informs us that "Israel, pursuing after a law of righteousness *[before God]* did not attain unto *that* law. Why? Because *they sought it*...by works" (Rom. 9:31f). But Paul had earlier said, "Now a righteousness of God apart from law has been manifested, being witnessed by the Law and the prophets *[in the O.T.]*, even a righteousness of God through faith in Jesus Christ for all those who believe" (Rom. 3.21f).

"A righteousness of God" (God's provision of righteousness) concerns a judicial righteousness pronounced by the righteous Judge. By it believers are adjudged as "Not guilty!" under the Law of sin and death. The well recognized scholar, N. T. Wright, has written as follows.

Paul's doctrine of justification is focused on the divine *law-court*. God, as judge, "finds in favor of," and hence acquits from their sin, those who believe in Jesus Christ. The word *justify* has this law-court as its metaphorical home base.[1]

This judicial righteousness is reckoned to (put to the account of) all who believe. "The righteous shall live by faith";[2] this has ever been the way of salvation for men. ("Shall live"—through resurrection and/or rapture—is in the future tense.)

In the Bible a law of faith (Rom. 3.27) was initially made known when God promised Abraham that he would have an offspring out of his own loins in his old age. Abraham received this promise more than 450 years before the Law of Moses was delivered to the Nation of Israel. Upon hearing this promise, Abraham "believed the LORD; and He reckoned it to him as righteousness" (Gen. 15.6).

The apostle Paul comments as follows on this law of faith as it applies to all who will believe God's Word.

> Rom. 4.20-25   [Abraham] did not stagger at the promise of God through unbelief, but was strong in faith—giving glory to God—21 being fully convinced that what He had promised, He was also able to perform. 22 And therefore "it was accounted[3] to him for righteousness." *[Paul is quoting Gen. 15.6.]*
>
> 23 Now it was not written for his sake alone that *[righteousness]* was imputed to him, 24 but also for us. It shall be imputed to those believing upon Him who raised up Jesus our Lord from the dead, 25 who was delivered up because of our offenses, and was raised for our justification.

---

[1] Excerpted from N. T. Wright's book, *Justification*, published by InterVarsity Press; page 12. Italics and internal quotation marks are Wright's.

[2] Hab. 2.4; Rom. 1.17; Gal. 3.11; Heb. 10.38.

[3] The words "accounted" (v. 22) and "imputed" (vv. 23,24) derive from the same Greek word, *logizomai*, and they mean "to put to one's account (as), or credit (as), or reckon (as)."

In his epistles to the believers in Rome, Galatia, and Ephesus, Paul went to great lengths to establish the fact that justification is imputed upon faith alone. Here is one of a number of examples.

> Eph. 2.8-10   For by grace you *[who were originally unbelievers]* have been saved *[viz., justified]* through faith, and that not of yourselves; it is the gift of God, 9 not of works, lest anyone should boast; 10 for we are His workmanship, having been created in Christ Jesus unto *[i.e., for the doing of]* good works, which God prepared beforehand that we should walk in them *[as believers]*."

The affirmations of truth in Eph. 2.8,9 engender no controversy among orthodox Christians. However, not a few of the saints become uneasy in a discussion of verse 10, perhaps being anxious about what that discussion may lead to. Therefore, I will have more to say on the matter of good works in our next section.

However, before closing out this section, let us notice something more that Paul has to say regarding justification by faith: again, with reference to the life of Abraham. "What then shall we say that Abraham…has found? For if Abraham was justified by works, he would have had something to boast about; but not before God. For what does the Scripture say? 'Abraham believed God, and it was accounted to him for righteousness'" (Rom. 4.1-3). Initial justification—our thereby being deemed as righteous with regard to the Law of sin and death—is God's gift reckoned according to faith, plus nothing. Hallelujah!

By Works

Let us return to Eph. 2.10: "For we are His workmanship, having been created in Christ Jesus unto *[i.e., for the doing of]* good works…." Now it must be admitted that what a believer should do and what he will do may prove to be differing realities in his life.

Bringing up the subject of works in the company of Christians might cause some of them to lower their eyebrows and squint, their lips becoming pursed in anticipation of what may follow. Some will resist a full hearing of what the N.T. has to say concerning their important relevance to salvation. This may be due to a dogged presupposition that any emphasis upon works is to place believers back under law—"Thou shalt" and "Thou shalt not."

"For [we] are not under law, but *[only]* under grace"—this is the singular assessment in the minds of many concerning Rom. 6.14. This is a skewed interpretation and a limited understanding of Paul's meaning in this verse. In consequence, many believers remain naïve with respect to how good works, or their absence, will ultimately effect our experience of salvation—viz., the salvation of our soul (1 Pet. 1.9-22). Untangling the confusion that abounds in certain circles concerning the doctrine of justification by works is important; we must have a right understanding of this doctrine in order to advance from faith to faith.

Faith and Works—Their Connection

Let us begin by observing, first, something that the apostle Paul says: "A man is not justified by works of law, but through faith of Christ Jesus" (Gal. 2.16). On the other hand, the apostle James says that "a man is justified by works and not by faith alone" (Jas. 2.24). How will we reconcile these two truths?

Let us notice something that James had previously said: "Even so faith, if it has not works, is dead, *being* by itself" (Jas. 2.17). (Death is not annihilation—as we shall see in Chapter 7—but a separation of things intended to remain conjoined.) Faith and works are meant to coexist in the life of every believer. Devoid of works the believer's faith is said to be dead: alone, by itself. In another place James says that "faith without works is barren" (Jas. 2.20).[4] The barren womb is not nonexistent; rather, it is useless and worthless as to its created purpose—dead in this sense.

---

[4] I conclude that "barren" (Greek, *argeé*), as opposed to "dead" (*nekros*), is correct—though the distinction hardly amounts to a difference in the end.

Resolving this apparent contradiction[5] between Paul's words and those of James comes through understanding that Paul (in Gal. 2.16, above) is speaking only about initial justification—being put legally right before God by faith. James, on the other hand (in Jas. 2.24, above), is speaking about justification by works that should be evidenced in a believer's life after he has been legally justified.

James goes on to say that "just as the body without a spirit is dead, so also faith without works is dead" (Jas. 2.26). Here, James is comparing a natural truth with a spiritual one. In the natural, a man is kept alive by a spirit (the breath) within him, and the departure of that spirit causes his body to become dead. The spiritual application is that works animate, keep alive, the faith of believers. If works are diminishing in a believer's life, so will his faith be diminishing. A man afflicted with pulmonary emphysema is experiencing diminishing breath, and his body is on its way to dying. If God's intended works diminish unto eventually vacating the life of a believer, his faith will become as dead.

As an aside, I will close out this subsection by noticing something that issues forth, not uncommonly, from the mouths of pulpiteers. They are often heard to say, "When God looks at you, all He sees is Christ." Some go even further: "When God looks at you, He does not see your sins; He only sees Christ in you." Such statements are responsible for bringing much misunderstanding into the imagination of their auditors. It would be far more correct to simply say, "When God looks at Christians, He sees His children." This is the believer's legal standing before the Father;[6] but his state of righteousness, his living a righteous life before God...this may be something of a different kind.

---

[5]   The following observation cannot be improved upon. "Whenever there is an apparent contradiction in the Word of God, diligent study, comparison and meditation will reveal a beautiful multi-faceted gem of biblical preciseness." This statement appears in *Should Christians Fear God Today?* by John Korsgaard, published by Crowne Publication, Inc.; p. 2.

[6]   God is the Father only of His children. While He is the Creator of all things in and by Christ, He cannot be owned as "Father" by any who are not His children. (Consider John 8.42ff; Rom. 9.8). The unbeliever is at enmity with God.

Be not deceived in this matter, beloved.

Works—Some are Valued, Some are Not

Jesus says, "Let your light so shine before men, that they may see your good works, and glorify your Father who is in heaven" (Matt. 5.16). There are many good works intended to bring glory to God: works like feeding the hungry; attending the sick; relieving the afflicted; visiting widows, the fatherless and those in prison, to name but a few. However, and regrettably, unbelievers oftentimes practice these things with more vigor than do believers. Since unbelievers, by definition, are oblivious of the truth that the one true God is the God and Father of our Lord Jesus Christ, how will He be glorified by them?

Whenever a Christian's endeavor is rooted in a desire to be seen and applauded by men; or when its object is some worldly gain; or if it is performed in order to acquire some sense of self-worth or goodness because one has done some seemingly good thing, it is practiced in vain before the Lord. Being motivated by any of these things, one may only expect to receive his reward now—from men (Matt. 6.2ff).

Paul admonishes believers: "Whatever you do in word or action, do all in the name of the Lord Jesus, giving thanks to God the Father through Him" (Col. 3.17). Our attitude should be that which the Lord described to His disciples: "When you have done all those things which you are commanded, say, 'We are unprofitable servants; we have *only* done that which it was our duty to do'" (Luke 17.7ff). This is safe ground. Let our love of, our obedience unto, and our dependence upon our Lord energize us unto good works as we look forward to His wondrous approbation in that future day—"Well done, good and faithful servant..." (Matt. 25.21ff).

God discerns the thoughts and intentions of the heart (Heb. 4.12). Good works, then, are to be adjudged by our Lord through His inside-out evaluation. Adam Clarke rightly notes in his *Commentary* on Col. 1.10: "Even a good work may be marred and rendered fruitless by being done improperly, out of season, or in a temper of mind that grieves the Holy Spirit."

Acceptable Righteousness

"Unless your righteousness exceeds the righteousness of the scribes and Pharisees, you will by no means enter the kingdom of heaven" (Matt. 5.20). These words of warning were addressed to disciples of our Lord Jesus.

For certain, the scribes and Pharisees lacked imputed righteousness; but furthermore, their works were motivated by self-interest; they desired to be esteemed as superior in godly piety by the common folk.

The standard of righteousness that should appertain to Christians ought to transcend that of the scribes and Pharisees. Jesus, in His Sermon on the Mount (Matthew, chapters 5-7) instructs believers about the many qualities of a spiritual kind that He hopes to find in us. (Please notice: no beckoning to "believe in Me" appears in that Sermon.)

Notwithstanding what Paul says to support his argument that initial justification (righteousness) is according to faith alone—using Abraham as an example (Rom. 4.1ff)—James uses this same man's life, and that of Rahab, to support his affirmation that acceptable, practical righteousness (justification) is thereafter adjudged according to works.

> James 2.20-25   But are you willing to recognize, you foolish fellow, that faith without works is barren? 21 Was not Abraham our father justified by works when he offered up Isaac his son on the altar? 22 You see that faith was working with his works; and, as a result of the works, faith was perfected; 23 and the Scripture was fulfilled which says, "and Abraham believed God, and it was reckoned to him as righteousness," and he was called the friend of God. 24 You see that a man is justified by works and not by faith alone.
>
> 25 In the same way, was not Rahab the harlot also justified by works when she received the messengers and sent them out another way? *[ref., Joshua, chapter 2.]*

Here, James is affirming that godly works should carry us on to the perfecting of faith (v. 22). "The Scripture was fulfilled" (v. 23)—meaning that it "was actually and fully realized."[7] Abraham's faith and that of Rahab was manifested in faith's action. "Actions are weighed" by God (1 Sam. 2.3); He is looking for the fruit of His planting.

Jesus' works were a perfect accomplishment of the Law (Matt. 5.17f), and He said, "My Father is working until now, and I Myself am working" (John 5.17). Can we see the symbiosis here?

Let us pause to notice just how Jesus was able to do what no other man has done. Jesus did nothing according to His own will. He did only the will of His Father; speaking the words He heard from the Father; doing what He saw the Father doing; always pleasing Him. It was the Father who was doing His works through the Son as the Son submitted Himself to doing only the will of His Father.[8]

This way of life led to Jesus' being justified and found worthy as a man.[9] Our works will likewise be justified only as we are "doers of His Word, and not hearers only, deceiving [our] own selves" (Jas. 1.22).

"Doers of His Word." Even an apostle was found blameworthy in his disobedience to God's word among Christians gathered at Antioch. In Galatians, chapter two, we read of Paul's reproving Peter and the Jewish Christians with him for their hypocrisy in eating with Gentile believers until the arrival of some Jewish believers sent by the apostle James; for when they arrived, Peter and his fellows quickly dissociated themselves from the Gentile Christians in fear of these Jewish brethren. Paul, therefore, rightly reproved Peter: see Gal. 2.16.

Jews were not allowed, under the Mosaic Law, to keep company with Gentiles; but Peter knew better (Acts 10.28). Peter was acting in the flesh and as under the Law—hence, Paul's reproof of his hypocrisy.

---

[7]   Marvin R. Vincent in *Vincent's N.T. Word Studies*.

[8]   See John 5.17-20,30a; 6.38; 7.16f; 8.28f; 12.49f; 14.10.

[9]   As a Servant of the Father: Acts 3.13ff; 4.30b; Phil. 2.7.

Concluding Thoughts

> Matt. 16.27   For the Son of Man will come in the glory of His Father with His angels, and then He will reward each according to *[the salvation received as the gift of God by grace through faith? No, for it will be according to]* his works.

> Luke 6.46   But why do you call Me "Lord, Lord," and do not the things which I say?[10]

J. D. Faust's quotation of Horatius Bonar is most appropriate in concluding our discussion of justification by works: "The sinner's *legal* position must be set right *[with God]* before his *moral* position can be touched."[11] A natural-born person is at enmity with God on both legal and moral grounds. And while this was the original circumstance of every believer (Eph. 2.1ff), we are now a new creation (2 Cor. 5.17).

The following are unarguable conclusions from God's Word.

1. A man must first be justified by faith before any of his works may be esteemed as righteous in God's sight.

2. Believers are not merely passive agents in the issues of this so great salvation into which we have entered (Heb. 2.3). The separate truths of God's sovereignty and man's responsibility are both established and preserved in the immutable Word of God.

3. Justification by both faith and works find their genesis in God's working in and through us.

With respect to this last point, Lang rightly observes:

> "Every virtue we possess,
>   And every victory won,

---

[10] In Matt. 7.21ff, Jesus says He will deny many who call Him "Lord, Lord"—in which passage believers, and not unbelievers, are the subjects of Jesus' denial.

[11] Excerpted from *The Rod: Will God Spare It?* by J. D. Faust, published by Schoettle Publishing Co., Inc.; p. 11. The quote is from *God's Way of Holiness* by Horatius Bonar, published by Moody Press; pp. 34,35. The bracketed, italicized words are mine; other italics are Bonar's.

> And every thought of holiness
> Are His alone."[12]

This quotation being indisputable, we must nevertheless yield ourselves to Him. It is necessary that every Christian should understand this: that any/every good thing in our life emanates from God, while every unrighteous thought and deed is a consequence of Satan's activity in influencing our mind and/or our flesh (human nature), usurping the grace and authority of the Spirit of God who dwells within us.

Justification by works, as we walk in faith, is a truth found throughout Scripture. Abraham's walk and ultimate perfecting of faith will be the focus of our next chapter; for he is the father of all who believe.[13]

---

[12] An excerpted quote found in G. H. Lang's book, *The Gospel of the Kingdom*, published by Schoettle Publishing Co., Inc.: page 34. (Whether these are Lang's words or those of another I do not know.)

[13] Rom. 4.11,16; Gal. 3.7ff.

Chapter 6

Faith—Its Working and Perfecting

The word "faith" is variably defined, depending upon the translation one reads, as "a substance of things hoped for, an evidence of things not seen" (Heb. 11.1). Vincent well says: "Faith apprehends as a real fact what is not revealed to the [natural] senses. It rests on that fact, acts upon it and is upheld by it in the face of all that seems to contradict it. Faith is a real [spiritual] seeing."[1]

When Peter confessed to Jesus, "You are the Christ, the Son of the living God," Jesus replied, "Blessed are you...for flesh and blood has not revealed *this* to you, but *[it has been revealed to you by]* My Father who is in heaven" (Matt. 16.16f).

Faith and the obedience due it is what we will examine and muse upon in the life of Abraham.

Abraham's Faith

The life of Abraham[2] demonstrates both failure and success—Scripture is always candid. Let us observe the progression of his walk of faith by considering what may be seen to be five Phases in his life.

---

[1] *Vincent's Word Studies in the New Testament*, by M. R. Vincent. Bracketed additions are mine, only to enhance what I believe is the author's full meaning.

[2] Abraham's original name was Abram, but it was later changed by God (Gen. 17.5).

Phase 1

Canaan was the Land of Promise destined to become Abraham's and his seed's.³ Prior to his leaving his hometown of Ur (in what is now southern Iraq) to go to dwell in the land of Canaan, God said to him, "Go forth from your country, and from your relatives…to the land which I will show you; and I will make you a great nation."⁴ Abram—accompanied by (at least) his father, Terah;⁵ his nephew, Lot; and his wife, Sarai—left Ur and settled in a city called Haran. When Abram was seventy-five years old, and after his father had died, he departed from Haran, accompanied by Sarai and Lot, on his way to the land of Canaan. Early in his sojourn in Canaan, "the LORD appeared to Abram and said, 'To your seed I will give this land'" (Gen. 12.7).

Up to this point the words "faith" and "believe" have not appeared in the Bible. Furthermore, we should notice that Abram's obedience of faith was both delayed and partial (he took Lot with him to Canaan)—a type, I believe, of Israel's lack of obedience under the Law.

Phase 2

More than ten years after having received the original promise from God, the LORD came to Abram in a vision. Abram asked Him, "Lord GOD, what will You give me, seeing I go childless, and the steward *[the acquired son or heir]* of my house is Eliezer of Damascus?" To this inquiry the LORD replied, "This one shall not be your heir, but one who will come from your own body shall be your heir." Immediately following the LORD's declaration we read, "And [Abram] believed the LORD; and He counted it to him as righteousness" (Gen. 15.1ff). Here we find the first and explicit notice of faith recorded in the Bible.

---

³ "Seed" ("offspring," singular; cp. Acts 7.5), which seed is later made known to be Christ (Gal. 3.16), though Abram was doubtless thinking only of a more imminent, natural offspring when he first heard God's promise.

⁴ Gen. 12.1-4; Act 7.2-4.

⁵ It is probable that Terah's extended family left Ur on their journey to Canaan.

However, we learn—albeit retrospectively in the N.T.—that Abram believed God's words when He appeared unto him back in Ur, perhaps some years before he left there on his journey toward Canaan (Heb. 11.8).[6]

Phase 3

Abram had been patient in faith for more than a decade, but his patience took a side-seat in the days following his receiving the promise of a son (an heir) recorded in Gen. 15.4. In this Phase we discover his reckoned faith becoming polluted by a work of the flesh.[7]

Abram's wife was barren. Therefore, at her suggestion, Abram went into her Egyptian maidservant, Hagar, in an attempt to bring forth the reality of God's promise. Hagar brought forth a son who was called Ishmael when Abram was eighty-six years old (Genesis 16).

Addressing the issue of the work of the flesh, Paul asks the believers in Galatia, rhetorically, "Having begun in *the* Spirit, are you now being made perfect by *the* flesh?" (Gal. 3.3).

As an aside, let us consider our own experience. Has any believer never discovered some promise or instruction in God's Word that has come to life in him personally—e.g., a call to the mission field—or had a personal vision from the Lord and then proceeded, in the anxious desires of the flesh, to attempt its accomplishment in his own strength?

Human nature is generally inclined to impatience; it is often unwilling to await the evidence of God's working out the accomplish-

---

[6] Likewise, the faith of Abel, Enoch, Noah, and Abraham's wife go unmentioned in the O.T.; but their faith is specifically acknowledged in the N.T. (Heb. 11.4ff). Hebrews 11.13ff informs us that "these all died in faith, not having received the promises; but, having seen them afar off, they were assured of them, embraced them, and confessed that they were strangers and pilgrims on the earth...." That all of these worthies died in faith evidences that they believed God's Word must be finally fulfilled in resurrection.

[7] "The flesh" often refers, here and elsewhere, to human nature and its separate activities outside of God's specific design.

ment of His Word or revelation. Perhaps the following experience in my own life will prove to be of some value here.

> I can readily recall a time, a few months before my conversion, when the Lord swept me up in a vision. (Yes, the Lord may grant visions to the unbeliever.) In that vision it was revealed to me that our family would relocate from our home in Connecticut to Maui.
>
> My wife and I went to Hawaii several months later. On the night of our arrival, I was brought to faith in Christ. One week later, in faith, we bought some property on Maui. That exercise of faith was confirmed in many ways by the Lord, though I cannot take space to go into their separate particulars.
>
> Almost immediately upon returning to Connecticut impatience took hold of me. For many months I did everything a man could do, with vigor and determination, to bring the vision into reality. I put the two houses we owned on the market and I began to aggressively advertise the availability of my business for sale. Lookers came and went, but no takers.
>
> About a year after I had been swept up in that vision not one thing had come to pass on the home front. Finally, while still being a babe in Christ, I went before the Lord in an abundance of tears and prayed something like this: "O Lord, I have been certain that the vision was from You, and I've been looking forward to its accomplishment. I've done everything I know to do to see it come into being, but nothing is succeeding, and I am frustrated and discouraged. So, I'm giving it up to You, and if You've changed Your mind I'll be content to stay right where I'm at for the rest of my life." (In all candidness, I'm not sure that I would have remained content indefinitely.)

Although I left the Realtor and the ads in place, my burden of discouragement was immediately lifted from me, and my ordinary life continued on in peace from that day forward.

Then, within a few months, things just began to happen. Both of our houses and my business were sold, effortlessly, in less than ninety days. Shortly thereafter our family was on its way to Maui. We arrived there only weeks after the house I had contracted to be built eighteen months earlier had been completed; its construction had undergone multiple delays. (God surely does know the end from the beginning [Isa. 46.10], and His timing is always perfect.)

Were it not for the sake of space and purpose, I could gladly add several more pages detailing the numerous workings of God that occurred during those last few months in Connecticut. Suffice to say this little. There is a major difference between a man working on his own, attempting to bring forth what he believes to be the will of God in his life, when compared to witnessing God's being at work in his circumstances. This is in order that a man might know God's great power to bring into reality things seemingly impossible. The principle is: "No flesh may glory [or, boast] before God" (1 Cor. 1.29).

While I am embarrassed to add the following addendum, it is the whole reason for having included the foregoing narrative.

Approaching two decades after our sovereign relocation to Maui, I became increasingly concerned about Y2K. I was thoroughly convinced that the fearful events predicted to occur after the clock struck 12:00 a.m. on January 1, 2000 would come to pass.

Attending only to the counsel of others, including the advice of many Christians, I undertook plans to relocate back to the Mainland.

Following our relocation to a place in rural, south-
west Missouri, we stored up foodstuffs, erected a wind
generator, installed solar panels, etc. But because I had
not sought the Lord's guidance in this plan, I found
myself fraught with exasperation and hardship from its
inception on into many months thereafter.

In utter repentance I finally went before the Lord
and confessed my absolute neglect of seeking His
guidance in this matter; and after a year or more He
restored my way in peace. Oh, how gracious He is.

God is ever "the God of patience" (Rom. 15.5); human nature
frequently tends to impatience. God is ever the Teacher of His children; but let us not be truant in His school of faith. Teaching is a
process over time, even in and through our impatience, and the weakness and failings of our human nature. The Word of God says, "[His]
strength is made perfect in [our] weakness" (2 Cor. 12.9). Pink observes
that "God's opportunity does not come until man's extremity is
reached."[8] These words are well spoken.

Returning our attention to this Phase 3 in Abram's walk, I would
add this. I find no passage in Scripture that records God's displeasure
or rebuke concerning what resulted from Abram's impatience unto his
acquiring a son. Abram needed to learn a lesson (as we all do) through
the consequences of his actions apart from waiting on God.[9]

Phase 4

Thirteen years after the birth of Ishmael, when Abraham was
ninety-nine years old, the LORD appeared to him again and declared
that He would give him a son out of his barren wife, Sarah. Abraham
laughed in amazement and said to himself, "Will a child be born to a

---

[8]   From *Gleanings in Genesis* by A.W. Pink, published by Moody Press: p. 183.

[9]   Hagar and Ishmael became a source of contention within Abraham's house,
      and Ishmael became a progenitor of Israel's enemies, even to this present day.

man one hundred years old? And will Sarah, who is ninety years old, bear a child?" Later, when Sarah overheard these words of the LORD repeated to Abraham, she likewise laughed. But, of course, a son was born of her, and his name was called Isaac (Gen., chapters 17; 18; 21).

Now what man, being ninety-nine years old, would expect to bring forth a son through a wife who was ninety years old? Perhaps only our oldest readers can truly empathize with Abraham's and Sarah's problem here, and how much participation in faith was required on their part; for they were beyond the time of sexual *joie de vie*, and Sarah had been barren all of her life. And yet, by faith in the Word of the LORD, they were both brought to willing cooperation according to God's good pleasure, and the child of promise was miraculously brought forth. "Is anything too difficult for the LORD?" (Gen. 18.14)

The years following Isaac's birth marked a turning point in Abraham's faith. They unveil to us the maturation and perfecting of his faith (as we will see next) when compared to that righteousness by faith without works which was first accredited to him in Gen. 15.6.

Phase 5

When Isaac was a lad (grown beyond childhood) God again appeared to Abraham and commanded him: "Take now your son, your only son,[10] whom you love, Isaac, and go to the land of Moriah, and offer him there as a burnt offering on one of the mountains of which I will tell you" (Gen 22.2ff).

Despite the fact that Abraham knew by then that God's promises to him were to continue forward through Isaac (and not through Ishmael), he was nevertheless instant in obedience and intention.

Before his ascent to the mount with Isaac, Abraham spoke these stunning words to the two young men who were accompanying them on their journey: "Stay here with the donkey, and I and the lad will go

---

[10] We understand from this statement that God had only ever had a certain son in view—Isaac, a type of the future Son, Jesus Christ: both miraculously born.

over there; and we will worship and *[we will]* return to you" (Gen. 22.5). Abraham was believing in God's resurrecting power (cp. Heb. 11.19).

We should pause to notice that Isaac—being yet unaware of Abraham's specific intention—asked his father at some point, "Father, where is the lamb for a burnt offering?" Abraham answered, "God will provide Himself the lamb for a burnt offering."[11] (Oh, how much could be said with regard to these words.)

Again, concerning Isaac: he is seen as a type of Christ (as Abraham is a type of the Father). Never once, like as with Christ, is it ever recorded in Scripture that Isaac protested against or resisted for one moment the determined plan of his father. Abraham's willingness and intention to sacrifice the son of his love was according to his full persuasion "that God was able to raise him up, even from the dead" (Heb. 11.19); for Abraham believed that God must and would fulfill His promises through Isaac.

The end of the narrative finds Abraham—knife in hand, on the brink of slaying his son—interrupted by these words spoken to him by an angel of the LORD: "Do not stretch out your hand against the lad, and do nothing to him; for now I know that you fear God, since you have not withheld your son, your only son, from Me" (Gen. 22.12). Upon hearing these words, "Abraham lifted his eyes and looked, and there behind him was a ram caught in a thicket by its horns. So Abraham went and took the ram, and offered it up for a burnt offering in place of his son" (Gen. 22.13).

His obedience of faith, recorded to encourage us, was the crowning achievement of Abraham's life of faith. In his words and actions we discover the perfecting of his faith (Jas. 2.21f).

For lack of space, I have passed over a goodly number of the faith-building particulars recorded in Genesis, chapters 15-22. Every reader

---

[11] Gen. 22.7,8. This statement in verse 8 can be literally understood to read, "God will see *[or*, behold*]* Himself a lamb for the burnt offering."

will be greatly profited in reading them; for they are typical of the varied experiences of the saints, and they have been recorded for our benefit. The main point to be understood from this brief overview of Abraham's life is this: the life of every believer is a journey. I would summarize our journey as follows.

Phase 1: A lack of godly obedience—a type of man under law, obedience being squelched by the flesh (Eph 2.1ff)

Phase 2: Faith reckoned without regard to works—a type of regeneration based upon faith alone (Eph. 2.8f)

Phase 3: The ineffectual efforts of the flesh—a type of "the old man" usurping the place of "the new man" in the life of a Christian (Eph. 4.22ff)

Phase 4: Cooperation in faith—a type of the prevailing of the new man in Christ (Col. 3.10)

Phase 5: Abandonment of all self-interest, in faith—a type of Christ's nature being formed and perfected in and through the believer's life (Jas. 2.22)

In closing out this review of Abraham's life, let us notice these same phases in Paul's life. As an unbeliever and a Law-keeping per-secutor of Christians, he was suddenly brought to faith in Jesus on his way to Damascus one day (Acts 9). Compare his remarks in Romans, chapter seven, with those in chapter eight, and in light of Gal. 2.20 and Phil. 1.21. Such a review suggests that Paul advanced from enslavement to human nature (even to God-deficient religion), to justification by faith, and then onward to the perfecting of that faith. (Paul was no timid, lackluster Christian, basking in the warrant of eternal life.)

Jesus was always and entirely dependent upon the life of His Father within Him; likewise, Paul became entirely dependent upon the life of Christ within him. He declared at one point: "I do not account my life of any value, nor as precious to myself" (Acts 20.24). This is to become our mindset as we go on to the perfecting of our faith (Matt. 5.48).

As an important, closing aside in our review of Abraham's life, let it be noticed that his faith was perfected in fear.[12]

Like a Coin

If faith were a coin, the one side would be stamped GOD WORKING IN US (Phil. 2.13) while the reverse side would be stamped OUR WORK OF FAITH (1 Thess. 1.11). The works that God has prepared for us to walk in are without profit if they do not find their source in and their power through the Holy Spirit. The acceptability of our works is according to our working them out in life as God works them in and through us.

To help make this truth more poignant, let us recall something that Jesus said to His disciples, and therefore to us who would be His disciples.[13] "Without Me you can do nothing *[of value Godward]*" (John 15.5). But here is something, mentioned earlier, that we frequently do not think about when reading of the wondrous words and works of our Lord. Jesus said that of Himself He could do nothing.[14] He told His antagonists at one point, "My Father is working until now, and I Myself am working *[according to the Father's working through Me, and not by My own designs]*" (John 5.17).

Our working by God's working in us are two sides of one coin.

Working by Faith in Peace

Perhaps you have received what you perceive to be a word from the Lord concerning a certain work you are to do. However, as you press on you may find yourself growing weary; you may even wonder at some point: "Am I really doing what God has called me to do?"

---

[12] Gen. 22.12; cp. Acts 9.31; Phil. 2.12.

[13] There is a difference between being a believer in Jesus and being His true disciple: see Mark 8.34,35; Luke 14.26,27. Discipleship exceeds redemption. Baptism, following upon faith, is God's first requirement of discipleship (Acts. 2.36-38). This truth often goes unmentioned in the preachings of evangelists.

[14] John 5.19,30; 8.28.

I would suggest an answer to such a question by raising another: "Are you experiencing the peace of God in this work?"

The work of Satan is "to steal, and kill, and destroy," and to dishearten you[15] in order that God's high calling for your life may be thwarted during your present days upon earth. However, if your troubles still find you having peace in your heart, you are on the right track; for Paul says to believers: "Let the peace of Christ rule in your hearts" (Col. 3.15). (Peace in faithfulness is a fruit of the Spirit [Gal. 5.22f].)

In this verse from Colossians, the words "let...rule"—rooted in one Greek word, *brabeus*—identify the activity of an umpire, a determiner. The peace of God is His comforting work in us, allowing us to know that any given work is pleasing to Him despite every obstacle. This is analogous to the umpire who declares, "Safe!" or "Out!" And though we may be nearly overcome by distress, persecution, or rejection along our way, we may still have assurance that our work is pleasing to the Lord if we have His peace within us.

Though I was originally reluctant to do so, please excuse me for adding another personal narrative that pertains to what has just been said concerning this peace of God.

> Years ago—while I was young in Christ, with much to learn—I was encouraged to contact a lawyer in order to get some financial redress in the matter of a serious injury I had sustained in a traffic accident.
>
> Some short time after legal proceedings were in process, I awoke one morning feeling an overwhelming sense of necessity to cease and desist in this matter. That very morning I went to my attorney's office, without an appointment, and instructed him to quit the suit. Even though I had had no qualms in this matter prior to that day, I experienced an unanticipated satisfaction and peace of heart in doing this.

---

[15] John 10.10; Gal. 6.9; Heb. 12.3.

Nevertheless, more than two decades later, while shopping in a local sporting goods store—being no longer a babe in Christ—I suffered an injury (one requiring surgery) due to the store's negligence and through no fault of my own. Considering the surgical expenses I was about to incur, I contacted an attorney who then filed a claim against the business's insurer.

During the weeks that followed, I found myself having no peace in the matter as I was continually mindful of the earlier event. Even though I tried to persuade myself that this episode was somehow different, there was no doubt in my mind about what I needed to do. Nevertheless, I procrastinated for many more months.

Finally, when I could no longer bear the anguish that accompanied my continued neglect, I contacted the lawyer and told him to abandon the claim. From that moment on peace of heart was again my portion.

My embarrassment in recording this second account of my frequent failings as a Christian is superseded only by my concern to make a point to each of God's beloved children. It is most unwise—even to our hurt as concerns our calling in Christ—to forget or ignore the clear, personal lessons that God has taught each of us in the past. I wonder if any of my readers may be presently embroiled in some conflict of conscience. If so, I hope that they will go before the throne of grace, in prayer and repentance, in order that they may find relief and rediscover the peace of God that surpasses all understanding.[16]

Jesus is the Good Shepherd. He will surely find His bleating, lost sheep—the ones who will cry out to Him for rescue—no matter what may have become their wrecked or perverse circumstance. He will recover, heal, and bring them back to the green pastures they once knew.

---

[16] Phil. 4.7; Heb. 4.16.

Chapter 7

Death and Glory

While most of what has preceded should, I hope, prove to be of no remarkable difficulty to mainline Christians, I must now take a fork off of the well-trodden road onto a path less traveled. Some may conclude that the doctrine posited hereafter is radically unorthodox. Nevertheless, I hope they will be like the Bereans and search the Scriptures to find out what is the truth in any matter (Acts 17.10f).

A misunderstanding of the proper connection between death and glory may take one astray from the faith "once for all delivered to the saints." Unprofitable and delusional are all of the traditions and assumptions of men that are not according to God's Word (Matt. 15.3).

Man was created in the image of God (Gen. 1.26f), and he is a tripartite being—"spirit, and soul, and body" (1 Thess. 5.23); he is not a bipartite being consisting only of body and soul, or body and spirit. While the words "spirit" and "soul"[1] may oftentimes appear to be undifferentiated in Scripture, God declares that they are separate things:

---

[1] The word "soul" is one translation of the Hebrew word *nephesh* and the Greek word *psuche. Psuche* is rendered nearly forty times as "life," and slightly less than sixty times as "soul" in the N.T. In Mark 8.35,36 both "life" and "soul" are translations of this one Greek word, *psuche.* In certain passages it would not be incorrect to understand *psuche* as "soul-life." In some places the Bible refers to men who are/were bodily alive as "souls"; at other times "soul" is simply a reference to a noncorporeal part of man.

things able to be divided, one from the other (Heb. 4.12). Since elaboration on their distinctions would take us far afield, it must suffice to simply say that one's soul is who one is as a person. It displays his personhood; it is one's self. The true essence of every living man is his indwelling soul, manifested to others through his spoken words and bodily activities. (Even after believers die physically, we are yet alive unto God;[2] and the "we" who are alive is with reference to our soul.)

The dividing asunder of a man's spirit, and soul, and body is called death. Death, from God's perspective, is not annihilation. Rather, it is the separation of things intended to remain conjoined, and this is the case whether the term "death" is used literally or metaphorically in the Bible. The following few examples of this Biblical perspective will support this affirmation.

- Genesis records that although Adam lived to be nine hundred and thirty years old, he experienced a very certain death in the day of his sin; he was separated from the personal, living presence of the LORD God.[3]

- A certain father beheld the return of his prodigal son and proclaimed, "This my son was dead and is alive again!" (Luke 15.24). Although the son had been as physically alive in his wasteful wanderings as he was upon his return to his father's house, their long separation was considered by his father to be as death.

- Paul writes that a widowed believer "who lives in *[self-indulgent]* pleasure is dead *[as to her communion with God]* even while she lives" (1 Tim. 5.5f).

It is most unfortunate that there are true believers who are holding fast to what—from a careful study of Scripture—is proven to be an erroneous expectation. They say: "Because I accepted Jesus in my heart

---

2   Luke 20.37,38; cp. John 11.26; Rev. 6.9; 20.4.

3   Gen. 2.17; 3.23f; 5.5.

at an ol' altar years ago, when I die I'm going to glory in heaven." A few are even heard to speculate that Saint Peter will be standing at heaven's gate to welcome them in on the day of their departure from this life. Many are anticipating being reunited with their loved ones and friends, in heaven, the moment after they die.

However, this is not to be our hope according to Paul; for he has summoned us to be "awaiting the blessed hope and appearing of the glory of our great God and Savior Jesus Christ" at His coming (Titus 2.11-13). This hope is not one of dying and of our naked soul then going directly to heaven's glory; rather, it anticipates resurrection (and /or rapture: 1 Thess. 4.15). Paul says the following in another place.

> 2 Cor. 5.2-4   For in this *[body]* we groan, earnestly desiring to be clothed with our habitation which is from heaven, 3 if indeed, being clothed, we shall not be found naked. 4 For we who are in this tent *[our present body]* do groan, being burdened, not because we want to be unclothed *[in death]*, but further clothed upon, that mortality may be swallowed up by life *[in resurrection and/ or rapture]*.

I am unable to find any explicit statement in the Bible that suggests that upon death the naked soul of any believer has ever ascended from its physical body directly up to heaven in glory. A future resurrection and/or rapture into the presence of the Lord is that for which we are to be awaiting and hoping. Many evangelists promote another notion; some even encourage their unbelieving auditors: "Buy your bus ticket to heaven at once." (Yes, I have heard this said.) Oh, how the Word of God is sometimes mishandled through errant preaching.

If the souls of those who die through Jesus ascend directly into heaven, why were some in Thessalonica sorrowing over the assumed fate of their departed fellows? Paul did not comfort them by saying that their dead loved ones were in heaven. Instead, he assured those blessed sorrowers that the faithful, having died through Jesus, will be resurrected and raptured to meet the Lord in the air (1 Thess. 4.13ff).

Our Lord and His apostles have informed us about what actually happens to those who die through Jesus—they fall asleep.[4] This sleep is not to be confused with a supposed, unconscious soul sleep put forth in the doctrine of Jehovah's Witnesses and some others.[5] The dead, to the contrary, are fully alive unto God as affirmed in Mark 12.26f and Luke 16.19-31; and John the Revelator wrote:

> Rev. 6.9-11   When [Jesus Christ] opened the fifth seal, I saw under the altar the souls of those who had been slain for the word of God and for the testimony which they held. 10 And they cried with a loud voice, saying, "How long, O Lord, holy and true, until You judge and avenge our blood on those who dwell on the earth?" 11 Then a white robe was given to each of them; and it was said to them that they should rest a little while longer, until both the number of their fellow servants and their brethren, who would be killed as they were, was completed.

The altar (under which these souls were seen to be) must, I presume, refer to the earth; for it was upon the earth that they were martyred. The book of Revelation was written years after Christ's ascension. Yet, these souls are seen to be very much alive, crying out to God from under that altar. It was in this place that they are told to "rest a little while longer."

The Greek word *hades* refers to the place of general confinement of the souls of the dead. Its location is downward, "in the heart of the earth," being the place into which the soul of Jesus descended for "three days and three nights" after His death, there to remain until His resurrection.[6] Very shortly after He was raised from the dead, Jesus appeared to Mary Magdalene—the first person to whom He showed

---

[4]   John 11.11-14; Acts 7.59,60; 1 Cor. 15.6; 1 Thess. 4.13-15.

[5]   Paul says our risen Lord "has become a firstfruits of those who have fallen asleep" (1 Cor. 15.20), "the pains of *His* death *[not of His dying]* having been loosed" (Act. 2.24). Pain is not experienced in unconsciousness.

[6]   Psa. 16.10; Matt. 12.40; Acts 2.27,31; Eph. 4.9,10.

Himself alive forevermore—and He emphatically declared to her, "I have not yet ascended to My Father" (John 20.17).

Hades downward location is confirmed even in the O.T. The patriarch, Jacob, distraught over the assumed death of his son, Joseph, said, "I will go down to sheol mourning for my son" (Gen. 37.35): *sheol*—the Hebrew equivalent of the Greek word *hades*—being likewise downward in location.[7] Also, following the death of the O.T. prophet Samuel, we read that he was later called up to counsel King Saul through the necromancy of a witch. Samuel asked on that occasion, "Why have you disturbed me by bringing me up?" (1 Sam. 28.11ff).

"Hades," being rendered as "hell" in some translations, tends to add confusion to confusion. Hades is not synonymous with the Lake of Fire (or, hell); for at the final reckoning both death and Hades will be cast into that Lake. No one whose name is found recorded in the Book of Life will find his eternal abode in that place (Rev. 20.14f).

There is a location within Hades known as "Paradise," and it is a place of rest separated from but in view of Hades' other portion of suffering (Luke 16.22ff).[8] This Paradise was the destination promised to one of the two criminals crucified alongside Jesus (Luke 23.43); and it is, undoubtedly, a place of rest for the departed (but living) souls of the righteous.[9]

Despite objections that may be raised by some, the speculation that departed, disembodied souls ascend directly (in glory) to heaven is

---

[7]   See Num. 16.33; Prov. 9.18; Isa. 5.14; 14.15; Ezek. 31.15-17 in the NASB.

[8]   In the Bible several different places are referred to as "Paradise"—the Garden of Eden (Gen. 2.8, in the Septuagint [LXX]); Ezek. 28.13); the Paradise of God wherein is the Tree of Life (Rev. 2.7); and, finally, the initial destination of the righteous upon their death (Luke 23.43). I am presently only concerned with the last mentioned Paradise. (This Paradise is perhaps in the center of Hades in light of Isa. 14.15 and Ezek. 32.23. And while Jesus descended into Paradise, He also entered into the darkest, tormenting portions of *sheol* [the pit; Hades]: cp. Acts. 2.27,31; Psa. 88; Isa. 44.23; Eph. 4.9.)

[9]   See Matt. 22.32; Mark 12.26f; Luke 20.37f.

annulled of all possibility by referring, first, to the second chapter of the book of Acts.

On the Day of Pentecost—ten days after Jesus ascended into heaven—Peter proclaimed the following to the multitude of his listeners: "Men and brethren, let me speak freely to you of the patriarch David, that he is both dead and buried, and his tomb is with us unto this day...For David did not ascend into the heavens" (Acts 2.29,34a). Let there be no confusion here; for the true essence of a man is not his body, but his living soul. David is dead and his soul has not ascended into heavenly glory. If David's soul has not ascended, have any others?

Next, let us notice the circumstance of the O.T. prophet, Daniel. "But as for you *[Daniel]*, go your way 'till the end *[viz., the end of your life]*; then you will enter into rest *[in Paradise]* and *[later]* rise again *[in the resurrection of the just]* for your allotted portion *[in the kingdom]* at the end of the days *[the end of these present days: "the end of the age" in the NASB]*" (Dan. 12.13). We should take careful notice of the sequence of these events—dying; then the soul's entering into rest (but not its immediate ascension into heaven); and finally, a future resurrection.

As a slight but interesting digression, I would mention that the constitution of man differs from that of angels (Heb. 1.7). Even though angels are permitted, at times, to manifest themselves to men in the form of a human body, it is not a body like ours.[10]

Until the ascension of the Lord Jesus in a resurrected body of flesh and bones (Luke 24.39), only spirit beings had occupied heaven; for this is the realm they are suited through creation to occupy. Human beings—in their present bodies, originally created from the dust of the earth—are not suited to any realm other than one earthly (1 Cor. 15. 48). We notice that even He who created all things—the Word (Jesus Christ)—was necessarily made like unto us in all things, in the likeness

---

[10] See Gen. 19.1-4; Heb. 13.2. Whatever their visible bodies may be composed of, they do not contain blood. Blood is the life of man's flesh; "the life of the flesh is in the blood" (Lev. 17.11). Angels cannot die (Luke 20.35,36).

of sinful flesh, in order to dwell as a true man among men.[11] It was not until He was raised from the dead that His physical body was fitted through resurrection to ascend to His Father and to be glorified.[12]

The only person who has ascended into the highest heaven after dying, and only after His bodily resurrection, is the Lord Jesus; for "no one has ascended into heaven except He who came down from heaven, that is, the Son of Man *who is in heaven*" (John 3.13).[13]

The souls of the righteous dead, presently at rest in Paradise, are consciously anticipating the day when "the Lord Himself will descend from heaven with a shout, with the voice of an archangel, and with the trumpet of God; and the dead in Christ will arise."[14] The heavenly calling of the deceased, righteous sons of God therefore necessitates their resurrection with an incorruptible, immortal, glorified body like that of our Lord (Phil. 3.21). Jesus is the pattern Son. Resurrection from death unto life should be the wonderful expectation of all the children of God; it will be His future act in the redemption of His own.

Whenever the teaching that one's naked soul ascends at death to a place on high is introduced, the whole of resurrection truth becomes disjointed, and it is not according to Christ. It would be helpful unto all correctness of doctrine if one will offer up a single verse of Scripture that expressly states that the immediate destination of the soul of a deceased believer is upward into heavenly glory. (See "Appendix A: Concerning Objections to My Views on Death and Glory," page 157.)

---

[11] John 1.14; Rom. 8.3; Phil. 2.7f; Col. 1.16; Heb. 2.3,17.

[12] John 1.1,14; 20.17; Rom. 8.3; Phil. 2.6ff; Heb. 2.14a,17.

[13] John's gospel was written years after Jesus' ascension. Therefore, these words in John 3.13 are undoubtedly John's own, even though recorded in red in red-lettered translations.

This is so because the words "has ascended" are in the perfect tense. This tense refers to "a condition resulting from an anterior occurrence...the result of the occurrence is seen to be 'present' or simultaneous with the time of speaking" (Wheeler's *Greek Syntax Notes*). Since Jesus was not then ascended, these words in John 3.13 cannot be His own.

[14] 1 Thess. 4.16; and notice Rev. 6.9-11.

Teachers and preachers who promote this unscriptural though popular assumption cripple and emasculate the great and wonderful significance of the doctrine of a future resurrection from death. That some may be doing so in ignorance is beside the point. I know first-hand of those who have been thoroughly instructed in the correct doctrine, but who have nevertheless put it away from themselves. Worse yet, the Lord may leave them in their present misunderstanding; for it is written, "Therefore, leaving the discussion of the elementary principles of Christ [*one of which is the doctrine of resurrection*], let us go on to perfection…And this we will do, if God permits" (Heb. 6.1ff).

"If God permits." This should bring a fearful reverence for the Word of Truth into the heart of every believer—especially teachers of the saints. How undermining are some of the vain, traditional doctrines of men. "Beware, lest anyone shall take you captive through philosophy and vain deceit, according to the tradition of men…" (Col. 2.8).

I suspect I have heard pulpiteers posit fifty times—most often at funerals—that the soul of a believer is transported to heaven upon death for every one time that resurrection is introduced as our faith-filled expectation.

The presumption that death immediately transports the soul of every believer into heaven's glory is not only naïve, but it may prove to be detrimental in the lives of many Christians. Such an assumption can easily lead one into complacency, the believer opting out of the race for the prize of the high, heavenly calling of God in Christ Jesus.[15] Not a few believers presume that being glorified together with Christ as His joint-heirs is an automatic warrant of God based solely upon regeneration. It is not; for Rom. 8.17 makes such heirship to be conditional. (We will consider this affirmation in later places.)

As mentioned in the opening paragraph, I have departed from what is, sadly, the main course of the doctrines of death and glory. I pray

---

[15] 1 Cor. 9.24ff; Phil. 3.14.

that no person called "Christian" will merely dismiss, out of hand, the view put forth above. Let us each become instructed in the way of God more perfectly through our own careful investigation of His Word.

Finally, I am left to wonder: "Why are we admonished to be looking for the appearing of God's Son, awaiting His coming from heaven in glory, if we are going unto Him, in glory, at death?"[16]

> Rev. 14.13 Blessed are the dead who die in the Lord... that they may rest from their labors, and their works follow them.

---

[16] Concerning our awaiting His appearing, see 1 Thess. 1.10; 1 Tim. 6.14f; 2 Tim. 4.1; Titus 2 13.

Chapter 8

The Age to Come—The Millennium

Leaving the controversy of our last chapter, let us move along to an-other—one that concerns the doctrine of the Millennium: the Age to come. The term "millennium"[1] has led to doctrinal contention among believers at various times in Christendom's history. This term will be the subject for review in this chapter.

While the age to come is referred to as "the Millennium" in many books and articles that I have read, this appellation invariably appears without any Biblical defense to undergird their writers' Millennial affir-mations. Consequently, while being fully persuaded of certain other truths put forth in those same writings I was, for some long time, unacquainted with any sound, exegetical[2] support that would undergird their capitalized use of this word.

These writers frequently and only define "the Millennium" as the "thousand years" mentioned in the opening verses of Revelation 20. This seemed inadequate and unconvincing to me, and such a meager offering, when trying to convey Millennial truth to others, will likely prove to be unpersuasive and may meet with stalwart resistance from

---

[1] "Millennium" is not a Biblical term. It derives from various interpretations of the phrase, "a..." or "the thousand years," appearing six times in Rev. 20.2-7.

[2] "Exegesis" means and refers to "the meticulous investigation and explanation of the meaning of Biblical passages," often with reference to the Hebrew and Greek texts.

strict opponents. However, the veracity of Millennial truth became clear and alive to me upon my own review of N.T. Greek texts.

Some readers may already be fully persuaded of the glorious truth of the Millennial Age of Christ's kingdom. Others, however, may be wholly unaware that there are millennial, doctrinal distinctions held within the Church. And finally, there are those in-between who find themselves totally confused by the variety of opinions they have been exposed to in the writings and preachings of men.

Before continuing, I wish to assure every reader that this subject is not being taken up simply to prove a point of doctrine; but I am persuaded that "the Millennium"—as I will define it in a Proposition near this chapter's end—can become a powerfully motivating hope for those pressing on to the glory into which we are being called.[3]

For the benefit of those readers who are unaware of or are confused about millennial doctrine, I will begin by comparing three widely held eschatological[4] views that have prevailed off and on over the centuries of Christendom's history. Each separate view differs entirely from and is in conflict with the other two views, and adherents of any one position are sometimes at variance with others of the same persuasion over certain details.

The following definitions may seem too broad-brushed to some readers; but it is only my intention to nonprejudicially summarize the general, doctrinal holdings of each group and their respective meanings in their use of the term "millennium," omitting notice of many details.

Premillennialism (Premills)

This doctrine teaches that a new and distinct age of time ("the Millennium") will be inaugurated upon the return of the Lord Jesus at

---

[3]   This hope, glory, and calling will be covered in later places.

[4]   *Eschatology* refers to doctrines concerning future/final things: e.g., the coming of the Lord, resurrection, rapture, judgment, etc.

the conclusion of this present, evil age: one that will intervene this age and the innumerable ages of eternity to follow thereafter.[5]

Amillennialism (Amills)

This group often prefers to be identified as "present..." or "realized millennialists." They see "a millennium" as having reference to Jesus Christ's present spiritual reign; that it is concurrent with our present Church age; and that it will continue until Christ's second coming at the end of this age. They further teach that at His second coming eternity will set in with no separate and literal (Millennial) age to fall between the end of this age and the beginning of the eternal ages.

Postmillennialism (Postmills)

Postmills believe that our present, evil world will eventually become so positively influenced through the spread of the gospel that after some very long but undefined period of transition nearly all the world will have become transformed by and under the influence of Christian doctrine. They refer to this long Christianized period of time (during this age) as "a millennial era." Postmills posit that during this Christianized era mankind will thrive and be at peace until its far end.

Then, they continue, Christ will return after a tribulation that will arise on the heels of this Christianized era, and that following His return the eternal ages will set in with no intervening (Millennial) age.

The differences in these several views are illustrated in "Chart 1: Millennialists Divided" on page 74. To summarize in words:

1. Amills and Postmills believe that a millennium
    a. is or will be a part of this present age; and that it
    b. will antedate (precede) Christ's second coming.

---

[5] The distinction between "Dispensational" and "Historic" Premillennialism is being passed over here, as discussing their unique differences will not contribute to my limited intentions in this chapter.

2. Premills hold that the Millennium

    a. will be a separate age that will follow upon a worldwide tribulation at the end of this present age, and that it will precede the setting in of the further, endless ages of eternity; and that it

    b. will be inaugurated at Christ's second coming upon the conclusion of our present, evil age.

Before going any further, I must affirm—even to the one who has a decided mind as to which of these mutually exclusive doctrines is correct—that I do not consider one's holding within this subject to be any test of orthodoxy. Some of the most brilliant and godly Christians to have ever graced the face of the earth have held to one or another of these views, though some have changed their position along their way. Though they cannot all be right, this in no way diminishes these believers' sterling value to the Christian community through their manner of life and their various writings handed down to us.

Those who hold a Premillennial view—including myself and many others—understand the N.T. to be identifying and distinguishing the Millennial Age as follows.

Proposition

That Age will be a specific, separate, manifest, future age of time: one that will commence upon the return of the Lord Jesus at the conclusion of this age. It will be an age to be followed by innumerable ages forever and ever.

It has seemed best to me to separate all of the above from the supporting documentation to be found in "Appendix B: Concerning the Ages" on page 161. I am doing this for two reasons.

1. Some, who may have been unaware of any millennial distinctions within the Church, may find themselves

thoughtfully stretched if they should choose to pause to review that detailed Appendix; they will need to petition the Lord for understanding.

2. Others, whose doctrinal position is already Premillennial, might prefer to simply move on to chapters that follow. (However, I would venture to say that their persuasion will be further confirmed by reviewing the material presented in that Appendix.)

Patient perusal of the information presented therein will, I pray, bring each reader into an initial or enhanced vision and hope concerning the glorious coming of our Lord and His kingdom, in order that we may all be pressing on toward God's highest purpose for having saved us in Christ in the first place.

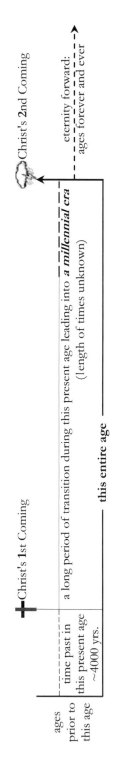

Chapter 9

Worthiness—An Introduction

In normal life, men may deem certain others to be worthy in some way, and perhaps rightfully so. Yet it is best for every Christian to always, personally, have the mindset of Jacob: "I am not worthy of all the loving-kindness and of all the faithfulness that You have shown unto Your servant" (Gen. 32.10). Jesus instructs His disciples with these words: "When you have done all those things which you are commanded, say, 'We are unprofitable servants; we have *only* done what was our duty to do'" (Luke 17.10). The psalmist, David, declares, "My soul shall make her boast *[only]* in the LORD (Psa. 34.2).

Such heartfelt attitudes will establish us on safe, spiritual ground.

Defining Worthiness

Several Greek words are translated a total of approximately fifty times in the N.T. as "worthy" or "accounted worthy." These words carry the same meaning in both Greek and English. They have reference to deservedness (or merit), brought into being as we are "transformed by the renewing of [our] mind" (Rom. 12.2), and as we move on to "fully pleasing [the Lord], being fruitful in every good work" (Col. 1.10).

Naturally-born men are—as if by definition—unworthy. They are at enmity with God, unsurrendered to Christ, and slaves to their fallen, sinful human nature (Eph. 2.1ff). And while it has pleased God to redeem a myriad of unworthy ones, many of these so blessed are living well beneath their calling.

A Matter of Time

Believers have been "freely justified as a gift by [God's] grace through the redemption that is in Christ Jesus" (Rom. 3.24). Justification (the imputation of righteousness) is God's gift to the unworthy (Rom. 6.23).

However, many born-again ones have been misled into thinking that upon regeneration God infused them with worthiness. This is not so. I am unable to find any specific notice in Scripture where God reckons any believer as worthy simply by virtue of his having been begotten of Him. Worthiness is not the result of simply being born again.[1]

A righteous standing with God upon regeneration occurs in a moment; worthiness of character and through our bringing forth the fruits of righteousness (2 Cor. 9.10) after being born again require time.

Along our way we are being called to "walk worthy of God, who is calling [us] into His own kingdom and glory" (1 Thess. 2.9ff). One may be called to be a participant in a certain event; yet he may, through disinterest and idle preoccupation with many things, be found unready when the event commences.[2]

Worthiness—Its N.T. Notice

Positive and negative notices of worthiness are recorded in many places in the N.T. Here are a few examples.

> Matt. 10.37,38   *[Jesus told His disciples,]* "He who loves father or mother more than Me is not worthy of Me.

---

[1]   Believers are said to be "in Christ Jesus who, from God, is made unto us… righteousness" (1 Cor. 1.30). This imputed righteousness (see footnote 3 on page 38) has to do with our being saved from the curse of the Law; but this is something different from worthiness in its godly, practical sense.

[2]   Cp. the parables of the Wedding Feast and the Ten Virgins (Matt. 22.1ff; 25.1ff).

And he who loves son or daughter more than Me is not worthy of Me. 38 And he who is not taking up his cross and following after Me is not worthy of Me."

Luke 20.35   But those who are counted worthy to attain that age, and the resurrection from the dead…

Col. 1.9,10   …walk worthy of the Lord, fully pleasing *Him*…

2 Thess. 1.4b,5,11,12 …counted worthy of the kingdom of God…that our God may count you worthy of this calling…

1 Tim. 5.18b The laborer is worthy of his wage.[3]

Being in a state of worthiness now is of great importance as we look forward to the future return of our Lord.

Christ—The Worthy One

We read in the book of Revelation: "Worthy is the Lamb who was slain to receive power and riches and wisdom, and strength and honor and glory and blessing!" (Rev. 5.12). Jesus' being supernaturally born as the Son of God (in flesh) is not the principal thing in view here.

As recorded by Paul, our Lord willingly divested Himself of His own eternal power and glory as God and was made in the likeness of sinful flesh, taking upon Himself the form of a servant as He dwelt among men.[4]

It cannot be overstressed: the name of the only begotten Son of God has not been exalted above every name simply based upon His Royal birth, but according to His conquest as the Son of Man. He has been exalted because of His love for and His willing submission to His Father's will with all of His heart, soul, mind and strength—as a man. It is because of His love and submission then that our Lord Jesus is exalted as a man of flesh and bones now in the highest heaven.

---

3 "His wage" or "his reward" (Greek, *misthos)*—parallel mention in Luke 10.7

4 Rom. 8.3; Phil. 2.7.

If this kind of love and submission was Jesus' pathway to glory, how can it not be the way for us?[5] But how may we attain unto such worthiness?

Worthiness and a Cross

The issue of worthiness is the issue of bearing a cross—not Jesus' cross, but our cross.[6] Jesus' cross was one of suffering and atonement; our cross is one of suffering only. Our cross-bearing necessitates the abandonment of sinful enterprises and forgoing the unnecessary, corrupting things of this world for His sake and the gospel's.[7] How many believers fall back through fear of rejection by others after trying to dissociate themselves from their bad behavior? How many cannot resist keeping up with the self-indulgent, unnecessary gains of the Joneses?[8]

We are not compelled to take up our cross. However, our Master emphatically declares: "Whoever does not bear his own cross and come after Me cannot be My disciple" (Luke 14.27).

A believer must surrender himself to Christ if he will ever take up and bear his own cross. Some have never taken it up; others have taken it up only to lay it down along the too difficult, too narrow way.

A cross is ever the place of death: the death of our self-life.

During the course of a long-term illness, disability, or extended misfortune in life, some may be heard to say, "Oh well, I'm just bearing

---

5   Matt. 10.24f; cp. Rev. 17.14.

6   It is "our cross" (*staurón autoú*) in Matt. 10.38; Mark 8.34; Luke 9.23; and "our own cross" (*staurón heautoú*) in Luke 14.27. Only two men ever bore Jesus' cross. The One bore it willingly; the other, Simon of Cyrene, was compelled to do so by Roman soldiers (Matt. 27.32).

7   Matt. 19.29; Mark 8.35; 10.29.

8   The things available in the world far exceed the necessities of life. Many early and present day Christians were and still are stripped even of life's necessities in their pursuit of the Master (Heb. 10.34). Avoiding unnecessary, worldly ambitions, allurements, and excesses can prove to be most difficult—especially in the land of the free.

my cross." Such a nonchalant lament would seem to indicate that the speaker has likely not taken up his cross. Things happen to all of us (though not outside the allowances of God): things that may have no specific origin in what is a consequence of following Christ.

However, the Lord can use any dreadful circumstance for His glory;[9] and a disciple's continued, confident confession in faith of the ultimate good intentions of God for him (Rom. 8.28), despite his troubles and sufferings, is something that the Lord must surely consider to be commendable.

Anecdotally, I once mentioned something to a phone-friend—a blind believer—and he replied, "I'll make a note about that and take care of it later." In all innocence I then asked him, "Does your wife later read such notes to you?" My friend broke out in hilarious, child-like laughter and said, "No. What I mean is that I will type a note to myself on my audible computer and bring it up later today." This brother is presently doing a fine work for the gospel's sake since becoming blinded many years ago in his youthful days of debauchery, and I have never heard him carry on about his disability. His life must surely give encouragement to many others besides me.

Worthiness—Christ's Provision

The worthiness of any man derives only from the working of Christ's life within him. Only by His inward work can we overcome adversity so that our soul may be kept in a worthy state before the Lord.[10]

How many of us, having often read the admonitions of Scripture, pause to beseech God for help in those (sometimes hidden) things of our heart and life made known to us as His Word divides our soul and spirit asunder (Heb. 4.12)? Do we cry out to Him?—"O Lord, help me

---

[9] See Jesus' explanation concerning the man born blind in John 9.1-3.

[10] We who believe are in a righteous standing with God as concerns the penalty of Law. But a worthy state as concerns our living a Christlike life before the eyes of Him with whom we have to do…this is a matter of a separate kind.

to lay down my life and pick up my cross. Help me to consider my present life as nothing in light of Your glorious, heavenly calling."

While "[our] help comes from the Lord" (Psa. 121.2), I have personally, and not infrequently, experienced a certain delay before I am able to see the evidence of God's response to my pleas for help. Sometimes months, even years of repeated petitioning pass by before I am aware that He has advanced me beyond a certain unrighteous thought or way in my life. God has His purposes in delay.

We are ever and always invited to continually "come to the throne of grace with boldness, in order that we may obtain mercy and find grace to help in time of need" (Heb. 4.16). We ought never to run and attempt to hide from God in whatever may be our wretched condition; for He will hear, and He is ever pleased with our importunity: our urgent, persistent solicitation of His gracious help (cp. Luke 11.8).

Dear saints of God, let us not grow weary. If He delays in answering our earnest petitions, let us remember that His ways are surely past finding out (Rom. 11.33). On the other hand, let us not become complacent in our present way, for we are all in desperate need—more than we may know—of Christ's continually working in us.

Dying to our self while yet living: this is something that only Christ can do in and for us.

> Isa. 33.2   O LORD, be gracious unto us; we wait for You. Be our arm *[our strength]* every morning, our salvation in the time of trouble.

The Way

As noticed above and as recorded in all four gospels, laying our soul-life (our *psuche*) aside in willing surrendering to Christ as we bear our own cross must be the way of all who would be His disciples; this is what the Lord is looking for. The principle is: first the suffering, then the glory (cp. 1 Pet. 1.10f).

Chapter 10

Worthiness—On That Day

Worthiness will be the final issue with respect to kingdom inheritance when Christ returns.

The Parable of the Talents (Matthew 25) and the Parable of the Minas (Luke 19) reveal the truth about Christ's reckoning with His servants (us) in a future day. These are parables both similar and different. My following comments are with reference to the Talents, though I will notice its important distinction from the Minas later in this chapter.

Parables are illustrations intended to teach a spiritual principle or truth through the use of familiar language and events. Whenever we meditate upon a parable we must first seek an answer to this question: "What is the central truth being put forth in this parable's contextual appearance?"

The Lord must open our ears to hear and understand His parables (Mark 4.33f); intelligence is not the issue here. To some their truths remain veiled, while by others they are understood (Matt. 13.13ff).

The Parable of the Talents

This is a parable pregnant with important meaning for us now as we look forward to that certain future day.

Please familiarize yourself with this parable in Matt. 25.14-30 before continuing on to my comments below.

- This parable concerns the kingdom of heaven,[1] and it was spoken in private to certain of Jesus' disciples[2] in what is known as His Olivet Discourse. It is intended to awaken every believer unto spiritual foresightedness.

- The central message in this parable is unmistakably clear. The lord of those servants (a type of our Lord) will one day return to reckon with them concerning their service to him during his long absence.

- There is no evidence that two of the three servants mentioned herein were truly his own, while the third one was not. Such conjecture on the part of many has led to considerable confusion. All three servants in this parable were their lord's own, and not inclusive of any member of the general citizenry. (Cp. Luke 19.14.)

- The "man traveling to a far country" must surely represent the Lord Jesus: the One who has gone into the highest heaven, being presently seated at the Father's right hand;[3] and He, like the lord of those servants, has been gone "a long time" (v. 19). If this lord is not intended to prefigure our Lord (and His return), this parable becomes an obscure and mysterious narrative.

- The only factor that determined how much was given to each servant was his unique and particular ability according to his master's knowledge of him individually (vv. 14,15). (As an aside: "God has dealt to each [believer] a measure of faith" (Rom. 12.3) so that we may

---

[1] While the words "the kingdom of heaven" do not introduce this parable in the Greek text, Jesus is continuing on from the Parable of the Ten Virgins where they do appear (Matt. 25.1). His theme is the same in both places—His coming, on which account we are to be always prepared.

[2] Matt. 24.3; cp. Mark 13.3.

[3] Acts 2.33; 5.31; Heb. 1.3b; 1 Pet. 3.22.

be of profit to Him and others;[4] but we are expected to use what He has given to us to serve His interests.)

Let us consider the following illustration from ordinary life.

> A man may give his wife a newfangled apple peeler as a gift and ask her to use it to make him a tasty apple pie: his favorite. Over the next many months and years his wife never makes him such a pie, though she occasionally makes him a peach pie, a pumpkin pie, and other kinds of pies, but never his requested favorite—and this despite his occasional reminders of the gift he had given to her. But his gift goes unused.
>
> It is through no lack of ability or provision that she has denied her husband of his good pleasure. She has merely done as she pleased.

This is but a simple parallel to the far more serious point being made in the Parable of the Talents.

- In verses 20-23, the lord's settling of accounts with the first two of his servants is made known. Three important things may be gleaned from these verses to encourage the faithful.

  1. These first two servants—though they began with differing numbers of talents—both doubled their number by putting them to use.

  2. As a result, they both received the exact same commendation from their lord, word for word: "Well done, good and faithful servant…Enter into the joy of your lord."

---

[4] This "measure of faith," or "the Word of God" given to us (John 17.14a)—i.e., "seed" (2 Cor. 9.10)—are like the talents; they are things which may be increased or multiplied: see 2 Cor. 10.15; Acts 6.7.

3. The good news in this parable should be plain
    enough. Christ has delivered His goods to His
    servants, us included. We may all gain an
    increase through diligent use of these goods,
    and be found rich in good works, thereby to be
    accounted worthy of His commendation and to
    receive the reward at our Lord's coming.[5]

• Finally, we come to see the calamitous end of the third
  servant in verses 24-29. As concerns his case, let us
  observe three things of grave significance.

1. The fact that he had "dug in the ground and hid
    his lord's money" displayed his utter worthless-
    ness in his lord's service during his absence (v.
    18). He, like his two fellow servants, had been
    given provision and opportunity. However, he
    chose to do nothing with his lord's talent, de-
    ciding rather to bury it, unseen and unem-
    ployed. (We all need to ask ourselves: "What am
    I doing with the Lord's provision?")

2. He tried to imply—as an excuse for his ne-
    glect—that he had been afraid of his own lord,
    whom he termed "a hard man" (v. 24). In his
    lord's reply to this bogus excuse this servant
    was sternly rebuked, being told that if it was
    indeed true that he feared his lord, this should
    have been all the more reason for him to have
    put his lord's money to use. (Are we walking in
    the proper fear of the Lord?)

    Because of his blatant disregard of the in-
    tended use of his lord's granting he is declared
    to be "a wicked and lazy servant" (v. 26).

---

[5] 1 Cor. 3.9-14; 2 John 8; Rev. 22.12.

3. The consequences of his neglect, which were two, are then made fully known. First, that which he had was taken from him; secondly, he was cast into outer darkness (vv. 28ff).[6]

I will summarize by saying this. We have each been given God's Word, or some specific gift(s) or talent(s) by our Lord. We are only called to trade in that which we have been given. But trade we must!

The Parable of the Minas is along a similar line.[7] In that parable one mina[8] was given to each of ten servants. Some gained more than others, and their resultant acknowledgment and reward varied accordingly. One servant did nothing with his mina, laying it away, to his great consequence. The contrast between these two parables illustrates that reward is proportioned according to [i] our ability and allotment, and [ii] our individual endeavor in service to the Master.

Closing Thoughts

The most popular summary of the parable of the Talents—a view put forth by many—is that the first two servants represent believers who will go into heaven's glory, while the third servant represents one of the Lord's own (or perhaps an unbeliever) consigned to eternal damnation

---

6   A discussion of what outer darkness represents will be passed over at this point, for it would require far too much unprofitable space to discuss the several opinions posited among Biblical scholars concerning its meaning. Suffice to say that this is a most dreadful consequence. And while I maintain that it does not pertain to eternal damnation in the Lake of Fire, this fact should be of little comfort to one who calls himself a Christian while persisting in sin; for he may be liable to receive the bad things referenced here.

7   The parables of the Talents, the Minas (Luke 19.12ff), the Prodigal Son (Luke 15.11ff), the Rich Young Rule (Mark 10.17ff), the Ten Virgins (Matt. 25.1ff), and others do not have saving faith upon regeneration in view. They refer to matters pertaining to the believer's faithfulness, service, readiness, and destiny since being saved. Paul's admonition to believers is this: "For you have been bought with a price: therefore glorify God in your body *[now]*" (1 Cor. 6.20).

8   A mina (or, a pound) was worth about "three month's salary" or "100 days' wages" according to footnotes in the NKJV and the NASB at Luke 19.13.

in the Lake of Fire. (I have previously given my reasons for rejecting any such notion as foolish imaginings.)

It has been God's intention from before the foundation of the world that man should rule His creation;[9] but fallen, then redeemed men will only rule under the headship of the Man, Christ Jesus. To be joint-heirs with Him in glory is God's call to all of His own, and it is the possibility made available to every believer. It is this possibility—and not the loss of eternal life—that every wicked, lazy Christian will be found to have forfeited on the day when the Lord reckons with him. Therefore, "Be ready, for the Son of Man is coming in that hour you do not expect" (Matt. 24.44).[10] D. M. Panton rightly observes: "All that contributes to holiness contributes to readiness."[11]

Our perusal of the Parable of the Talents discloses the truth about the reward to be either received or forfeited (or worse) in that future day; this would seem to be incontrovertible. Therefore, we ought to each ponder the following questions.

- "Am I using my talent(s) to the profit of the Lord, or only to my own profit in the world?"

- "Have I become spiritually lazy through a preoccupation with worldly things and the affairs of this life: my business, my desire for the baubles of the world, my hobbies, or my wanderlusts?"

- "Am I being about my Father's business?"

---

[9] Gen. 1.27,28; Eph. 1.4ff; Rev. 11.15.

[10] In the Greek, "Be ready" (*gínesthe hétoimoi*) is an imperative command, and it is in the middle voice, meaning (literally) "make yourselves ready."

[11] A quote lifted from Panton's book, *Rapture*, published by Schoettle Publishing Co., Inc.; p. 62.

Chapter 11

Worthiness—Addressing Uncertainties and Misgivings

> 2 Cor. 5.10 For we *[believers]* must all appear[1] before the judgment seat of Christ, that each one may receive the things done in the body, according to what he has done, whether good or bad.

Paul explicitly and succinctly presents the judgment seat of Christ to believers in his second epistle to the Corinthians. We can see how this verse is altogether consistent with the central message of the Parable of the Talents discussed in our previous chapter. Many other cautionary admonitions—addressed not to the world, but to believers—can be found in both the gospels and the epistles, as we shall soon see.

When preachers, teachers, and commentators expound upon our opening verse, they oftentimes focus on the Lord's future recompense for our well-doing (the "good"), while minimizing or neglecting any notice of the "bad" mentioned in this Corinthians passage. They frequently suggest something like this: "There is a crown to be received or not to be received at the judgment seat; you should hope to obtain that reward." This simple conclusion tends to emasculate 2 Cor. 5.10 of its intended potency; for Paul immediately continues: "Therefore, *[personally]* knowing the fear of the Lord, we persuade men *[concerning judgment]*."

---

[1] "Appear," (Greek, *faneerootheénai*)—"be exposed openly before all others."

N.T. warnings to the saints will be covered in Chapter 17; but because many Christians resist the notion of a believer receiving anything bad from the hand of the Judge, our Lord Jesus, I will open up the subject in this earlier place. As always, every proposition put forth by men, including my own, must be tried in the light of Scripture.

Let us take notice of a warning addressed to these same Corinthian believers in Paul's first letter to them. (It would be well to have your Bible opened since certain verses, not excerpted herein, will be referenced as we continue along.)

> 1 Cor. 6.9-11a   Do you not know that *the* unrighteous will not inherit the kingdom of God? Do not be deceived! Neither fornicators, nor idolaters, nor adulterers, nor homosexuals, nor sodomites, 10 nor thieves, nor covetous, nor drunkards, nor revilers, nor extortioners will inherit the kingdom of God. 11 And such were some of you....

In most translations, verse 9 is rendered as "...the unrighteous will not inherit...." And because verse 11 begins by saying, "such were some of you," many Christians who read verses 9-11 are led astray into thinking that our present passage has reference only to unbelievers. The following points will hopefully correct this false assumption.

- The definite article, "the," is italicized in this rendering from First Corinthians (above) because it does not appear in the Greek text. The use of the definite article in Greek is oftentimes of significance; for it frequently identifies and/or limits the someone or the something in view. Compare, for example, the general request, "Get me a box" (i.e., any box), with the more specific request, "Get me the box" (i.e., a specific box).

- If one will refer back to 1 Cor. 6.1 in his own Bible he will read of "the unrighteous," where the definite article ("the") is included. In that verse "the unrighteous" are unbelievers involved in a corrupt, worldly (legal) system; they are being contrasted with "the saints" (Christians) in that same verse. But beginning in verse 6, Paul is pointing out unrighteous behavior among believers in the Corinthian church; and his reproof of their unrighteousness leads right into verse 9, where no definite article appears in the Greek text. Verse 9 should be read as "…unrighteous ones…"—referring to any and all who are practicing unrighteousness.[2]

- Paul's corrective exclamation, "Do not be deceived!" (v. 9), is addressed to believers who thought (and still do think) that inheritance of the kingdom is a warrant of God based solely upon being born again. This is simply not so. What Paul is saying here is this: "Christians, do not be so deceived; for no person who is practicing unrighteousness will inherit the kingdom."

- There are, undeniably, children of God who are ensnared in one or more of the transgressions mentioned in verses 9 and 10. These transgressions are identified elsewhere in Scripture as "works of the flesh."[3]

- Paul's takes notice of the ungodly estate in which these believers did originally abide (v. 11). But let us who know the way of righteousness not become entangled again in the pollutions of the world. Let us not, as did the saved Israelites, turn our hearts to go back to Egypt:[4] a type of enslavement among the ungodly.

Two passages which shed light on the issues of our work of faith and our judgment are the following.

---

[2] Notice that 1 Cor. 6.9ff has nothing to do with the loss of eternal life; its focus is upon loss (forfeiture) of inheritance of the kingdom of God.

[3] Gal. 5.19ff; cp. Eph. 5.5,6.

[4] Num. 14.3f; Acts 7.39f.

> Eph. 6.5-8   Bondservants *[viz., Christians]*, be obedient to those who are your masters according to the flesh, with fear and trembling, in sincerity of heart, as to Christ; 6 not with eye-service, as men-pleasers, but as servants of Christ, doing the will of God from the heart, 7 with goodwill doing service, as unto the Lord, and not to men, 8 knowing that whatever good anyone does, he will receive the same from the Lord, whether he is a slave or free.

> Col. 3.23-25   And whatever you *[Christians]* do, do it heartily, as to the Lord and not to men, 24 knowing that from the Lord you will receive the reward of the inheritance; for you serve the Lord Christ. 25 But the *one* doing wrong will receive *unto himself* the consequences of the wrong which he has done, and without partiality.

Both passages emphasize that a believer is called to perform his doings as unto the Lord; he is not called to be a man-pleaser.[5] However, in the Colossians' citation we discover that the believer, if he be a wrongdoer, "will receive the consequences of the wrong which he has done:" viz., the bad things mentioned in our opening excerpt from Second Corinthians.

At this point some Christian will doubtless protest: "Aren't we all assured in 1 Thess. 5.23,24 that our whole spirit, and soul, and body will be preserved blameless in the presence of our Lord Jesus; and will He who calls us not be faithful to perform it?"

The objector fails to understand that 1 Thess. 5.23,24 must be read in the more extended context in which it appears: verses 12-24. (I will not take space to record these verses; for the reader with an opened Bible may examine them in their entirety.)

In 1 Thess. 5.12-22, we read a long list of things that we ought to practice or avoid during our lifetime as a believer. In light of their mention, allow me to draw our attention slightly aside for a moment.

---

[5]   "The fear of man brings a snare" (Prov. 29.25).

One of the two criminals dying alongside Jesus made this final request of Him: "Lord, remember me when You come into Your kingdom." This scoundrel lacked baptism and was absent of any good works; yet Jesus nevertheless assured him: "Today you shall be with Me in Paradise *[based upon your faith alone]*." (Notice, however, that the Lord's reply made no mention of His kingdom [Luke 23.42f].)

The theme of the N.T. is not our dying and then, as some say, our soul's ascending directly into heaven. Rather, its emphasis is upon our living by Christ as we prepare ourselves for and await His promised return. Most of us will live years, perhaps decades, beyond the time of our having been brought to faith in Jesus. Will we ignore the benefit of these additional years of life in contrast to the lack of even one more day for the criminal noticed above? Will we idle our life away?

Continuing our aside, another question seems germane. Will one receive special high honors for services done as a member of some worldly society on the day of his initiation? Of course not. Months or years of fidelity are first required. Likewise, after becoming numbered among the spiritual society of the redeemed, development of worthiness to be acknowledged by Christ will require time: time during which God will test and prove our allegiance to Him as He leads us onward to our inheritance and "the salvation of our souls."[6]

If godly character diminishes or fails to increase in the life of one begotten of God, then it is evident that such a one is quenching the Spirit of grace, walking according to the flesh, and (perhaps) that his or her faith is receding into barrenness (Jas. 2.20).

Let us now turn our attention back to First Thessalonians, chapter five. Immediately following his long list of things that believers ought and ought not to practice (vv. 12-22), Paul makes his personal wish known to/for the Thessalonians (and therefore to/for us): that they may be wholly sanctified, their whole spirit, and soul, and body being

---

[6] See 1 Pet. 1.3-9; Jas. 1.21. Soul-salvation has reference to reigning in Millennial glory with Christ.

preserved blameless in the presence of the Lord (v. 23). Then, and finally, he emphatically notes: "Faithful *is* the *One* calling you, who also will do *it*" (v. 24)—i.e., God will bring this to pass.

How may we harmonize [i] Paul's wish that we may be found sanctified (holy) and blameless in the presence of our Lord (v. 23) with [ii] the certainty that God will ultimately bring our sanctification and blamelessness into being (v. 24)? Here is a "wish" versus a "certainty."

(Do you recall my earlier mention of apparent contradictions that some seem to find within the Word of God? [Recall footnote 5 on page 41.] I have affirmed that all Scripture must be accepted as His immutable words of truth, whether or not our mind can presently harmonize their seeming mutual exclusivity.)

Something that Paul wrote to the Colossians will help us to resolve the difficulty presented in our two-part question just above.

> Col. 1.21-23   And you, who were once alienated and enemies in your mind by wicked works, He has now reconciled 22 in the body of [Christ's] flesh through death, to present you holy, and blameless, and above reproach before Himself—23 if indeed you abide in the faith, founded and steadfast, and not drifting away from the hope of the gospel which you heard....

"If" is a significant word here and elsewhere in Scripture. In 1 Thess. 5.24, it is affirmed that God will present us sanctified (holy) and blameless in the presence of the Lord. However, in Colossians this same end is seen to be upon condition: "if indeed." Therefore, I conclude that God will present us holy and blameless at least in the further ages of eternity (see Eph. 2.7). However, the conditional "if" of Col. 1.23 has reference to the Millennial Age.

Therefore, I conclude: Whether God will do as He has promised is not in question; it is, rather, a question of when and how He will do it.

The question raised earlier by our protester (back on page 90) suggests that he may be supposing one or both of two things. First, that having been brought to life through faith in Jesus Christ on some occasion—thereby having become one of the redeemed—all is presently and always well with his soul. Secondly, that there will be no differentiation among believers in the ages to come: that all believers will, at last, be found to be of equal status. I contend that such assumptions are grave errors, and I would further suggest that they will prove to be stumbling blocks in a believer's present walk.

Worthiness of resurrection and rapture unto kingdom inheritance "is not a gift, but a prize to be won, in the strength of the Lord, by the fruits of faith, conduct and works after conversion" (G. H. Pember).[7]

May we all be asking ourselves the following questions.

- "Am I harkening unto God's calling in the fear of the Lord?"[8]
- "Is my life manifesting the fruit of the Spirit?"[9]
- "Am I redeeming the time?"[10]

If the fruit of the Spirit is not emerging from and increasing in our lives as believers, or if our spiritual growth becomes stunted, by what means and at what time will God honor His warrant to present us holy and blameless and beyond reproach in His sight? Another has written, "Death works no magic upon character."[11] Sanctification—now, or when?[12]—this appears to be the question before us. Oh, how serious is this question, beloved?

---

[7] This quote by G. H. Pember is lifted from Panton's book, *Rapture*, published by Schoettle Publishing Co., Inc.; p. 46.

[8] Psa. 111.10a; Prov. 1.7; 10.27; 14.27; 19.23; Acts 9.31.

[9] Gal. 5.22f; Eph. 5.9.

[10] Eph. 5.16; Col. 4.5.

[11] From a footnote on page 59 in D. M. Panton's book, *The Judgment Seat of Christ*, published by Schoettle Publishing Co., Inc.

[12] Judgment (Heb. 9.27) seems to be determined before or immediately upon death (Luke 16.20; 2 Tim. 4.8; Rev. 6.9ff).

Chapter 12

Worthiness—With Respect to the Kingdom

Up to this point the term "eternal life" has appeared many times in this writing, but only with reference to its being the irrevocable gift of God. However, Paul writes to Titus that God "saved us…in order that having been justified *[saved]* by his grace, we might become[1] heirs according to *the* hope of eternal life" (Titus 3.5ff). Here we read that we have been saved unto a specific hope of inheritance. This hope of eternal life—"the hope of His calling" (Eph. 1.10—is not to be confused with our present, unalterable possession of eternal life (see John 3.36a).

Let us notice something that opens up Paul's writing to Titus.

> Titus 1.1,2   Paul, a servant of God and an apostle of Jesus Christ for the faith of God's elect and the knowledge of the truth that leads to godliness—2 *[a faith and knowledge resting]* upon a hope of eternal life, which God, who cannot lie, promised before *the* ages began.

Notice that Paul couples "godliness" in verse 1 with "hope of eternal life" in verse 2. The word "hope," in its N.T. usage, does not

---

[1] The Greek word *geneethoómen*, rendered as "we might become," is in the subjunctive mood. In *Greek for the Rest of Us* by William D. Mounce, published by Zondervan, we learn on his page 186 that the subjunctive mood very often "does not describe what is but what may (or might) be…it is the mood not of reality but of possibility (or probability)." Parentheses are Mounce's.

imply some sentimental wish. Rather, the word (here) connotes a joyful expectation of something good.

As I begin this chapter, I will interject an aside that has relevance to our present subject. Christians called Calvinists and others called Arminians have long been in a dispute over the issue of salvation. Arminians say that though we may have been saved on some occasion, there is a danger of our losing this salvation—though they sincerely wish that none of us should come to such an end. On the other hand, Calvinists nonapologetically declare, "Once saved, always saved."

Which is correct? In fact, they are both right and wrong. When the focus of their disagreement is upon being born again the Calvinists are correct. (They say one's being born, either physically or spiritually, does not involve anything one does of himself, and that anyone born cannot be unborn.) However, when the Arminian claims that our salvation may be lost, he is correct, but only as this loss has reference to a forfeiture of inheritance in Christ's Millennial kingdom. The dispute between Calvinists and Arminians is reconciled in the whole counsel of God.

Will anyone suggest that Paul had some doubt about his having received the irrevocable gift of eternal life while, at the same time, continually hoping that he wouldn't lose it—he himself having been the chief proponent of the doctrine of security? Never. In what sense, then, was Paul in fear of being disqualified (1 Cor. 9.27)? His fear concerned the possibility of not inheriting eternal life in the age to come (the Millennium); it did not appertain to the loss of eternal life in the further ages of eternity.

It will be my burden to support this view in our present chapter.

Inheriting Eternal Life

We know that a man becomes an heir of God's eternal life through faith alone, whereupon he has eternal life (John 3.36a). Only as being such an heir is any additional inheritance made available to him in Christ (the testator of God).

Notice what Paul commands (saved) Timothy to do: "Fight the good fight of faith; lay hold upon the eternal life into which you were called" (1 Tim. 6.12). The Greek word *epilaboú*, translated here as "lay hold upon," means "to seize upon, lay hold of, i.e. to struggle to obtain" (Thayer). Would anyone be called to struggle to lay hold of something that he presently, irrevocably possesses? No. There is, therefore, a more excellent aspect of eternal life that a Christian is to further lay hold of, taking care that no one robs him of it (see Col. 2.18).

The free, present possession of eternal life differs from inheriting it in the next Age. Inheritance of eternal life is noticed in Matt. 19, Mark 10, and Luke 10 and 18. Reviewing Mark's account will help us to understand our present subject of inheriting eternal life.

> Mark 10.15,17-30 *[Jesus, speaking in the presence of His disciples, said,]* "Assuredly, I say to you, whoever does not receive the kingdom of God as a little child will by no means enter it"…
>
> …17 Now as He was going out on the road, one came running, knelt before Him, and asked Him, "Good Teacher, what may I do in order that I might inherit eternal life?"
>
> 18 So Jesus said to him, "Why do you call Me good? No one is good but One, that is, God. 19 You know the commandments: 'Do not commit adultery,' 'Do not murder,' 'Do not steal,' 'Do not bear false witness,' 'Do not defraud,' 'Honor your father and your mother.'"
>
> 20 And he answered and said to Him, "Teacher, all these things I have kept from my youthful age."
>
> 21 Then Jesus, looking at him, loved him, and said to him, "One thing you lack: Go your way, sell whatever you have and give to the poor, and you will have treasure in heaven; and come, follow Me."
>
> 22 But he was sad at this word, and went away sorrowful, for he had great possessions.
>
> 23 Then Jesus looked around and said to His disciples, "How hard it is for those who have riches to enter the kingdom of God." 24 And the disciples were astonished at His words. But Jesus answered again and

said to them, "Children, how hard it is for those who trust in riches to enter the kingdom of God. 25 It is easier for a camel to go through the eye of a needle than for a rich man to enter the kingdom of God."

26 And they were greatly astonished, saying among themselves, "Who then can be saved?"

27 But Jesus looked at them and said, "With men it is impossible, but not with God; for with God all things are possible."

28 Then Peter began to say to Him, "See, we have left all and followed You."

29 So Jesus answered and said, "Assuredly, I say to you, there is no one who has left house or brothers or sisters or father or mother or wife or children or lands, for My sake and the gospel's, 30 who shall not receive a hundredfold now in this time—houses and brothers and sisters and mothers and children and lands, with persecutions—and in the age to come, eternal life.

A number of important things are revealed in this narrative.

- First, we see in verse 15 that Jesus has the kingdom on His mind and in His mouth, as always.

- Next, I would suggest that the inquirer of verse 17—commonly referred to as "the rich young ruler"—was already a believer. I say this for the following reason.

  In verse 21, Jesus "looking at him, loved him." The love of God is declared in Scripture only with respect to His own children.[2] I am unable to find a passage in the Bible where either the Father or the Son declares His love to unbelievers.[3] To the contrary, see John 3.36b.

  If anyone will object because John 3.16 says, "God so loved the world [kosmos]...," I would suggest that he check John 17.9 where Jesus says, "I pray for them [His

---

[2] E.g., Deut. 7.7f; Prov. 8.17; John 13.1,34; 14.21,23; 15.9,10; 16.27.

[3] In Rom. 5.8 and Eph. 2.4f, believers are being addressed. That God has always loved us is declared to us after we have been begotten of Him.

disciples]; I do not pray for the world *[kosmos]*." Notwithstanding this fact, all who come to faith in Jesus were (unknowingly) drawn to Him by God's love (John 6.44).

- Nothing in Mark 10.17ff has anything to do with coming to first faith in Christ and receiving the gift of eternal life apart from works. In fact, works are the only matter under consideration in this passage. Therefore, I am compelled to conclude that this account only has to do with a believer's being reckoned as worthy by Christ according as his work of faith shall be demonstrated.

- The issue of works (vv. 19-21), and of entering the kingdom (four times in vv. 15,23-25), and of receiving eternal life in the age to come (v. 30) are all connected.[4] They all pertain to answering the young ruler's question: "What may I do in order that I might inherit eternal life?" (Notice the Q&A in Luke 10.25ff.)

  If this man is unsaved, then the Good Teacher is telling him that if he will give up his wealth, distribute it to the poor, and follow Him, he will have treasure in heaven (v. 21). Is this the way unto regeneration? Certainly not. It is faith that redeems, while obedience to God's Law and Christ's commands lead to inheritance.

  A believer's worthiness with respect to inheritance is the only matter in view in this passage.

- Works, inheritance of the kingdom, and being saved are all interrelated in our present excerpt.

  (As an aside, let us wonder: "What shall we say about Jesus' statement in Mark 16.16?—'He who has believed, and has been baptized, shall be saved; but he

---

[4] In this collection of verses, "the kingdom…" (cp. Matt. 19.23,24) and "the age to come" refer to the Millennial kingdom: one which will be entered through inheritance, as a reward.

who has not believed shall be condemned.'" Baptism is a work of righteousness [Matt. 3.13ff]. So, what does the future hold for the one who believes, but ignores baptism? This is an important, kingdom question.)

- We can see that to "be saved" does not always and only have to do with regeneration. Such is the case in Mark 10.26, where to "be saved" is not a reference to being born again, but to an abundant entrance into Christ's kingdom.

An Abundant Entrance

With reference to this abundant entrance, let us move on to consider what Peter adds to our understanding of the importance of our endeavors in light of Millennial truth, though not apart from the grace of God working in us.

> 2 Pet. 1.1-11   Simon Peter, a servant and an apostle of Jesus Christ, to those who have received a like-precious faith with us in a righteousness of our God and Savior Jesus Christ.
>
> 2 May grace and peace be multiplied to you in a full knowledge of God and of Jesus our Lord, 3 according as Christ's divine power has given to us all things that pertain to life and godliness, through the full knowledge of Christ Who has called us to His own glory and virtue;[5] 4 whereby He has given to us exceedingly great and precious promises, in order that through them you might become partakers of the divine nature, having escaped the corruption that is in the world through lust.
>
> 5 And for this very reason, giving all diligence, add to your faith moral excellence, to moral excellence knowledge, 6 to knowledge self-control, to self-control patience, to patience godliness, 7 to godliness brotherly

---

[5]   Some translations read, "by…" or "through His own glory and virtue." I believe that "to…" (KJV) is the better rendering here in light of 1 Thess. 2.11f; 2 Thess. 2.14; and 1 Pet. 5.10—which verses will be noticed shortly.

affection, and to brotherly affection love. 8 For these things existing in you and abounding make *you* neither barren nor unfruitful in the full knowledge of our Lord Jesus Christ. 9 For he who lacks these things is blind, unable to see what is far off, having forgotten the cleansing from his old sins.

10 Therefore, brethren, rather be even more diligent to make your calling and election sure, for if you do these things you will never stumble; 11 for in this way an entrance will be abundantly supplied to you into the eternal kingdom of our Lord and Savior Jesus Christ.

Important truths are on display in this passage.

- Peter begins by identifying himself with all believers. He then immediately goes on in verse 2 to express, as an apostle, his wish for them (and for us): that grace and peace may be multiplied to us in a full knowledge of God and of Jesus our Lord. This full knowledge (Greek, *epignosis*) is a higher than normal knowledge; it is not simply knowing about something or someone. Many know about Christ, but relatively few know Him?

- In verses 3 and 4, Peter informs us of what God has done for us in Christ; He has given us "all things that pertain to life and godliness," including "exceedingly great and precious promises."

  These assurances are put forth "so that by them [we] might become partakers of His divine nature" (v. 4).[6] This wondrous calling is further confirmed by Paul when he exhorts us to "walk worthy of God, the *One* calling [us] into His own kingdom and glory" (1 Thess. 2.11f). Peter says elsewhere, "But may the God of all grace, who has called you into His eternal glory in Christ Jesus…" (1 Pet. 5.10).

---

[6] "Might become" (*géneesthe*): subjunctive mood. See footnote 1, above.

Who can even imagine what such an experience may be like?

- In verses 5-8, Peter's attention turns to what is our duty. We are to give all diligence to adding the following seven things to our faith—moral excellence; knowledge; self-control; patience (steadfast perseverance); godliness (godlike character); brotherly affection; and love. Again, a purpose is given: that we may be found neither barren nor unfruitful (v. 8). God is always looking for fruits of righteousness to appear out of His planting.[7]

  Notice, beloved, that the seven things recorded in verses 5-7 are to be added to our faith; they are not things that were poured into us upon our regeneration. "Regeneration is the first essential...but it is not the last."[8] Our calling and election can only be made sure as we persevere now in this obedience, enabled by His grace; but we must avail ourselves of this grace.

  If one is neglectful in this matter he will not come to a full knowledge of Christ (v. 8); the light he thinks is in him may prove to be great darkness (cp. Matt. 6.22f).

- Moving on to verse 9, we hear Peter giving a warning— that if one is lacking in the virtues Peter has just noted, he is blind and forgetful with respect to his past and to "what is [presently] far off," but coming.

- In verse 10, Peter encourages us—that if we are diligent in our faith we will never stumble (or fall).[9]

---

[7] Notice Mark 4.20; Rom. 7.4f; Phil. 1.10,11.

[8] From Panton's *Rapture*; published by Schoettle Publishing Co.; Inc; p. 34.

[9] Though we all stumble along our way, our stumbling, followed by repentance, is not what Peter has in view here. He is speaking of a continued abiding in some stumbling, not followed by repentance, that, if it persists, might lead to one's final disqualification of receiving the prize: see Paul's concern in 1 Cor. 9.24-27.

- Finally, we come to Peter's grand crescendo in verse 11 —that in doing these things "an entrance will be abundantly supplied to [us] into the eternal kingdom of our Lord and Savior Jesus Christ."

This abundant entrance into Christ's eternal kingdom has reference to first entering (to inherit) His temporal, Millennial kingdom.

We examined the difference between a gift (irrevocable) and a reward (conditional) in Chapter 3. In Chapter 8 and Appendix B, we learned of the difference between Christ's one, temporal, Millennial kingdom and His eternal kingdom which will continue into the innumerable ages that will follow thereafter. Finally, the issue of our worthiness in the hope of being glorified together with Christ in His kingdom has been thoroughly reviewed in the last several chapters.

Entering Millennial glory finds its great moment in 2 Pet. 1.11.

Paul said something (previously noticed) to Timothy in 2 Tim. 2.6 —something that pertains to this abundant entrance. "The hardworking farmer must be first *[before others]* to partake of the crops."

A Christian may fail to become a first-partaker by not tending the farmland of grace present in Christ, thereby becoming unfruitful, and having no increase to present to the Lord on that Day. (Recall the parables of the Talents and the Minas.)

I pray, beloved, that you have received this kingdom message as a little child (Mark 10.15); for what sorrow neglect may bring upon those who are lazy or disinterested. Can we even imagine what it would be like to find this proffered kingdom a forfeit?

It is to those who are accounted as worthy through the use of the means made available by God in Christ that the reward of the inheritance will be abundantly supplied. God is calling each of His redeemed ones to become joint-heirs with Christ in His Millennial reign. Notice that "those who are *[to be associated]* with [Christ] are called, and chosen, and faithful" (Rev. 17.14).

Chart 2, appearing on the next page, illustrates and summarizes what is my thesis concerning eternal life and the reward of the inheritance.

The second coming of Christ is to be our (farsighted) blessed hope as we await "the appearing of the glory of our great God and Savior Jesus Christ" (Titus 2.13). The nearsighted may be lusting after the things of this age; or they may be reigning in it, or "lording it over" the saints (which Paul denounces[10]); or they may simply be satisfied with the temporal blessings being received in this day. (Please notice that even unbelievers are blessed by God [Matt. 5.45b].)

The farsighted are looking fixedly—even in the suffering of trials, tragedy, and persecutions—unto future things as yet unseen (2 Cor. 4.18). They are holding on to a hope of an abundant entrance into Christ's kingdom.

Let us be encouraged, beloved—yea! even captivated—by God's assurance that "eye has not seen, nor ear heard, nor has *the* heart of *a* man imagined the things which God has prepared for those who love Him" (1 Cor. 2.9). Dear saints of God, let us all "lay hold of eternal life, into which [we] have been called," so that "we may have confidence and not be put to shame before Him in His coming."[11]

> Luke 21.36   Watch therefore, and pray always that you may be counted worthy [or, may prevail] to escape all these things that will come to pass [on the whole earth], and to be set [in safety] before the Son of Man.

Escape how? I will address this question in our next chapter.

---

[10] See 1 Cor. 4.8ff; 1 Pet. 5.2ff.

[11] 1 Tim. 6.12ff...1 John 2.28.

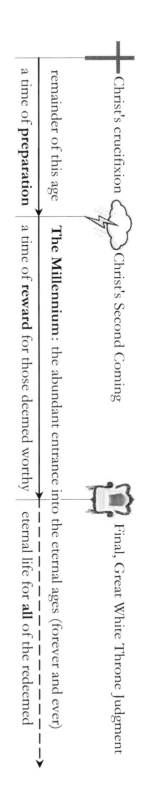

Christ's crucifixion

remainder of this age

a time of **preparation**

Christ's Second Coming

The Millennium: the abundant entrance into the eternal ages (forever and ever)

a time of **reward** for those deemed worthy

Final, Great White Throne Judgment

eternal life for **all** of the redeemed

Chapter 13

Resurrection and Rapture

No work of this kind can ignore notice of the subjects of resurrection and rapture[1] (r/r).

Conflicting r/r doctrines have been in controversy among believers throughout much of the history of Christianity. One view has become preeminent, only to be replaced by another, and then another.

In studying these differing r/r doctrines I have come to the following two conclusions.

1. Christians, who have subscribed to a particular r/r doctrine, even for centuries, have tended to resemble lemmings. They share a mass mentality without any real knowledge of Scripture that would either confirm or invalidate their understanding. They hold to their doctrine simply because it is what they have always believed—their church or denomination believes it, therefore they believe it.

---

[1] The word "rapture" is not a Biblical word. It derives from the appearance of the word *rapio* in the Latin Bible, but it is rendered as "caught up" in most translations of 1 Thess. 4.17. In current teachings the use of the term "rapture" is often focused upon living believers only. However, Paul associates resurrection of the dead in Christ with rapture in 1 Thess. 4.16,17: "the dead in Christ will first rise; then we who are alive and remain shall be caught up *[raptured]* together with them in the clouds to meet the Lord in the air."

2. When contending against other views in support of
    their own—whether in a public setting or in their
    writings—Christian academics often put forth a grand
    display of head knowledge, and their objective often-
    times seems to be to prove that their position is the ex-
    clusively correct one.

Entire books, readily available, have been devoted to the subject of
r/r. Though many are primarily presentations of their author's own
personal persuasion,[2] I do not intend to choose a side in this writing.
My objectives in addressing this topic are limited to two.

1. First, I will present some basic, general information
    concerning three major r/r theories that have been at
    odds with one another within Christendom over some
    long time; then I will notice one lesser known view. I
    am presenting this material because many who hold to
    some certain doctrine of r/r are frequently unaware that
    other, contrary doctrines even exist.

    I will define some language used in r/r discussions
    under the heading, "Definition of Terms."

2. Second, and most importantly, I hope that every reader
    will muse upon the question of whether watchfulness,
    readiness, and worthiness may have any important bear-
    ing upon one's hope of rapture.[3]

    "Questions...," introduced at this chapter's end, are
    intended to stimulate one's thinking along this line.

---

[2] I highly recommend a book entitled *Contemporary Options in Eschatology, A Study
of the Millennium* by Millard J. Erickson, published by Baker Book House. It is
for all intents and purposes an unbiased writing, and a thorough, fairly easy to
read treatment of various millennial and r/r doctrines. Its Table of Contents
allows the reader to quickly find just what he or she is interested in.

[3] Rapture of the living is the main concern among Christians today. Therefore,
my comments in this chapter will be more focused on this aspect of r/r
doctrines.

Be assured, beloved—this topic is not being taken up to tickle the intellect, or to prove the correctness of one specific theory, or to disparage any of them.

When we conclude this overview, I hope that you may have discovered something which will prove to be of practical value in your spiritual life: something that will arouse you to greater, present, heartfelt moral and observable uprightness of life. For if there is nothing of such value to be found in any of these doctrines of r/r, then we ought to dismiss all interest in the subject and simply, nonchalantly maintain an attitude of *que sera sera*. However, I am personally convinced that such a mindset may lead to our loss of something precious.

Before moving on to "Definition of Terms," I wish to affirm my conviction that one's view concerning r/r is not a test of orthodoxy. Some of the most godly and well instructed saints have held to differing views on this subject, though some have changed their ground along their way.

Definition of Terms

The following terms are admittedly broadly defined and limited in scope, overlooking the subdivisions and schisms that exist within each view. Nevertheless, they are adequate and impartial definitions of each term.

Millennialists Verses Tribulationists

In Chapter 8, we learned about the distinctives that divide Pre-, A- and Postmillennialists; how the term "millennium" is defined and communicated by these respective camps of believers was the issue discussed therein. Our present review focuses upon Premill doctrines.

Premillennial Pre-, Mid- and Post-tribulationists are at odds with one another over a different matter. These three are divided over the question of when the r/r and the second coming of Christ will occur with respect to a period of time referred to as "the Tribulation."

The Tribulation of Premillennialism

Present-day Premillennialists are united in a futuristic view of (a soon coming) end-time, worldwide tribulation. They understand from Scripture that turmoil will progress to catastrophe and overwhelm this present, evil age in its final days. These horrific troubles, they posit, are consistent with what Jesus foretold would finally result in "great tribulation, such as has not been since the beginning of the world until this time, no, nor ever shall be" (Matt. 24.21).[4]

At the end of this Great Tribulation, Premills hold that Christ will personally return onto the earth to establish His Millennial kingdom. All Premills are in agreement on these matters.

But then differences arise among them: differences pertaining to the timing of the r/r and the "coming" or the "presence" of Christ[5] with respect to this future period of Tribulation. This matter of timing finds Premills divided (primarily, but not exclusively) into one of three tribulation camps.

Pre-tribulation rapture theory (Pre-trib)

In its general and present-day presentation, Premillennial Pre-tribulationism teaches the following.

- Approximately seven years before His future return onto the earth, the Lord Jesus will leave His Father's throne and come concealed in clouds into the air (our sky), unseen at that time by the unbelieving world.

---

[4] As there are disagreements over millennial doctrines, so there are disagreements over tribulation doctrines. Pre-, A-, and Postmills have separate views on the issue of tribulation. Present-day Premills refer to "the Tribulation" as a future event but, at the same time, they contend that its advent is imminent.

[5] The Greek word *parousia* is variably understood to mean the "coming" or the "presence" of Christ. The debate over which rendering is more correct oftentimes leads to hot disputes among Biblical scholars. Suffice to say that context must be the decider in each occurrence of this Greek word.

- Upon His arrival in those clouds the Church (consisting of all born-again believers)[6] will be caught up (raptured) into Christ's presence, there to remain in order to be examined before His judgment seat. Previously raptured ones will then return to earth with Christ at His manifest second coming some seven years after this r/r.

- When the Lord Jesus returns to earth He will enforce judgment upon the nations and establish His Millennial kingdom.

Mid-tribulation rapture theory (Mid-trib)

Mid-tribs generally hold that the r/r will occur in the details just described under the Pre-tribulation rapture theory, but they posit that the time of this r/r will be midway through the seven-year Tribulation: i.e., approximately 3½ years prior to Christ's coming upon the earth.

Post-tribulation rapture theory (Post-trib)

Post-tribs contend that no r/r of believers will occur until the time of Christ's second (and only) coming upon the conclusion of the Great Tribulation. They go on to say that at His return all believers, dead and living, will be resurrected and/or raptured into His presence in clouds, and return to earth with Him shortly thereafter. Then, as in the previous two views, Christ will judge the nations and establish His Millennial kingdom.

R/R Timeline

The differences in timing that distinguish these Premill doctrines are illustrated in the timeline appearing as "Chart 3…" on page 117.

---

[6] When Pre-tribs use the word "Church," they seem not to be referring to some Christians, but to all Christians, living and dead—"The Church, whose punishment has been borne by Christ." This quotation is representative of the view of Pre-tribs; it appears in Chapter Thirteen of *Is The Rapture Next?,* by Leon Wood (a Pre-tribulationist), published by Zondervan; page unrecalled.

The Coming of the Lord

Christ's presence (or coming) relates directly to the timing of the r/r event in each of the above doctrinal holdings. For the Pre-tribs and Mid-tribs, His coming will first occur (invisibly to the world) some differing number of years prior to the close of the Great Tribulation. According to their teachings, Christ first comes for His church, and later with His church at the conclusion of the Great Tribulation.

However, Post-tribs teach that Christ's one and only coming will be manifested to every eye (Rev. 1.7), and that it will occur upon the conclusion of the Great Tribulation.

Pre-tribs and Post-tribs are at opposite ends of the spectrum of r/r timing. Mid-trib theology is not a mediator between these other two views. Each theory excludes the possibility of any correctness of the other two.

Timing— Its Importance to Believers

The moment of rapture with respect to the Tribulation should be of vital importance if any believers may be found alive and remaining into any portion of those awful days: see 1 Thess. 4.15ff. Rapture before, during, or after the Tribulation is the bone of contention among Premills; and the question of just when the rapture will occur is the centerpiece of each tribulation doctrine. With this important issue of timing in mind, let us review what has been said above in other words.

- Pre-tribs hold that all Christians who are living upon the earth when the seven years of Tribulation are about to set in will suddenly and unexpectedly be rapt (caught up) in advance of it into Christ's presence in the air, thereby sparing all living Christians from any of the dreadful events to follow upon the earth during the next seven years (cp. Luke 21.36). Pre-tribs further teach that the rapture could occur at any moment.

- According to Mid-trib teachings, living Christians will experience significant, personal persecutions and woes during the Tribulation at the hands of the ungodly until its midpoint. The Mid-trib rapture, they say, will spare living (raptured) believers from the more horrific events of its latter half: the Great Tribulation.

- Post-tribs believe that living believers will enter the Tribulation, and that some will remain throughout its entirety, though they are frank to acknowledge that many will be martyred for their testimony of Jesus during those years. As already noted, they teach that no r/r will occur until the finale of the Great Tribulation.

To Say A Bit More . . .

While Premillennial Pre-tribulationism may be the majority view among Protestants in our present day,[7] I trust that every reader understands that in all things the dominance of any one opinion does not, in and of itself, validate its correctness according to Scripture.

In listening to and reading the writings of many, the question concerning one's worthiness seems to find no dogmatic emphasis in the current teaching of an imminent r/r by Pre-tribs. Mid-tribs deal with this issue, but somewhat obscurely. Post-tribs, in emphasizing martyrdom, give more specific notice to worthiness; but they posit that believers will enter into the entirety of the Tribulation. (Pre-tribs will embrace none of this, while Mid-tribs will allow half of it.)

The Question of Worthiness With Respect to Rapture

My main concern remains: Do watchfulness, readiness, and worthiness have any relevant bearing upon one's expectation of rapture? I will put

---

[7] Catholic doctrine is historically and traditionally Amillennial.

forth the following few thoughts and questions upon which each reader may muse, regardless of what may be his present r/r persuasion.

- Many Christians are suffering little, if at all, for the sake of their faith. Yet Paul says, "…through many tribulations we must enter into the kingdom of God" (Acts 14.22). Absent the fruits of righteousness and the testimony of their mouths, the family, friends, and colleagues of many believers may not even be aware of their faith in Christ. In light of Acts 14.22, upon what basis may they be anticipating imminent rapture?

- Since tribulation can and should be of benefit to Christians,[8] will God deny its profit through rapture of lax or carnal believers? "Affliction is a dark room in which God develops some of His loveliest negatives"[9]

- Can we conclude that readiness has no bearing upon rapture in light of Jesus' command to "Watch *[be alert]* …and pray always, in order that you may be accounted worthy to escape all these things that are about to be coming to pass" (Luke 21.36)? There are numerous N.T. passages admonishing us to be always ready, sober, and spiritually awake. Concerning what? Escaping the hour of earth's trial through rapture, I presume.

- In the extreme, suppose that at Christ's coming some born-again believers are truly backslidden—some lying upon a bed of fornication, others perhaps involved in different ungodly behaviors. Should they expect to be suddenly rapt into Christ's presence, thereby being saved from the awful days of Tribulation?

---

[8] In Rom. 5.1-4, Paul reassures Christians that "tribulation produces patience; and patience, character; and character, hope." Surely, such resultant traits will contribute to one's becoming worthy of Christ. (Cp. also Heb. 12.9-11.)

[9] From D. M. Panton's book, *Rapture*, published by Schoettle Publishing; p. 28.

- A comparison of the spiritual condition of each of two churches in Revelation, chapter 3, is well worth contemplating as we conclude; for their distinction is marked.

> Rev. 3.10 *[to the Philadelphian church Jesus says]* "Because you have kept My command to persevere, I also will keep you from the hour of trial which shall come upon the whole world, to test those who dwell on the earth."

> Rev. 3.15,16 *[to the Laodicean church He says]* "I know your works, that you are neither cold nor hot. I could wish you were cold or hot. 16 So then, because you are lukewarm, and neither cold nor hot, I will vomit you out of My mouth."

Because the faithful Philadelphian believers will be kept from the hour of trial, while the unrepentant Laodicean believers will be vomited out of His mouth, can we see how the matter of readiness will bear upon the issue of rapture and inheritance of Millennial joy?

Another R/R Possibility

There is a lesser known doctrine referred to as Partial, or Select, or Multiple Rapture; its basic propositions are as follows.

Only persevering, watchful, praying believers will escape, be kept from, (at least) the (Great) Tribulation through early rapture; the rest will be left to enter thereinto.[10] Their remaining on earth to experience the increasingly dreadful persecutions and sufferings of the (Great) Tribulation will, hopefully, lead to their godly transformation. As this may occur, they will be raptured, at least upon the manifestation of our Lord—if not before—as He is about to return onto the earth. In this teaching the issues of worthiness and rapture appear to be reconciled.

---

[10] We read in Rev. 2.22: "Behold, I cast her *[Jezebel, a symbolic name: v. 20]* into a bed, and them that commit adultery with her *[viz., redeemed ones in the church in Thyatira]* into great tribulation, except *[unless]* they repent of her works."

Without taking notice of their varied and specific holdings I can say that there have been many noteworthy saints who have promulgated the general doctrine of Partial Rapture. A list of their names and some of their writings would include the following.

- Watchman Nee: *The King and the Kingdom of Heaven*

- Robert Govett: *Entrance Into The Kingdom; How Interpret The Apocalypse?* and his *Kingdom Studies*

- D. M. Panton: *Rapture*

- G. H. Lang: *The Revelation of Jesus Christ*; *Firstfruits and Harvest*; and his *Firstborn Sons, Their Rights and Risks*

- Others: Hudson Taylor, G. H. Pember, G. Campbell Morgan, Robert Chapman, George N. H. Peters, Joseph A. Seiss, A. B. Simpson, John Wilkinson, etc.

Regardless of your current holding, beloved, I pray that none of us will be numbered among those believers overcome,[11] so that "whenever He may be manifested *[appear]* we may have confidence, and not be put to shame before Him in His coming" (1 John 2.28). "Be ready," "Be awake," "Watch, and pray always"—these are the admonitions of Scripture unto all believers.[12]

My conclusion on our subject of r/r is this: the time of the rapture is not as important as is our being found watchful, ready and worthy whenever it may occur—even if it may occur in the next moment.

I pray that the present affairs of life may not usurp our being continually on the watch and ready, praying always, as we anticipate in hope the day of our resurrection and/or rapture unto inheriting the kingdom.

---

[11] The possibility of failing to overcome is clearly the implication in Christ's letters to the seven churches in Revelation, chapters 2 and 3.

[12] See Matt. 13.33-37; Luke 12.40; 21.36; Rom. 13.11f; 1 Cor. 15.33f.

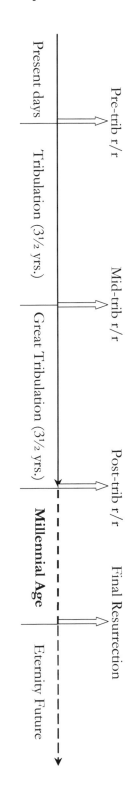

Chapter 14

Qualified Unto Inheritance

> Col. 1.7-12   …walk worthy of the Lord…who has qualified us unto *[becoming]* the partaker of the inheritance of the saints in the Light.

Let us muse together to become persuaded of this wonderful, momentous truth of our having been qualified to receive the inheritance.

Inheritance—Its Risks and Reward

Calling to mind some O.T. background will help us to better understand the subject of New Covenant inheritance.

Inheritance Under the Mosaic Covenant

Under the Mosaic Covenant the Israelites were to enter the Land promised to their fathers—the land of the Canaanites—for the purpose of possessing (inheriting) it. The LORD spoke through Moses saying, "You shall inherit their land, and I will give it to you to possess, a land flowing with milk and honey" (Lev. 20.24).[1] The O.T. links possession with inheritance of/in the Land dozens of times.[2]

---

[1]   This Land promise was first made known to the patriarchs (Gen. 15.7; 28.4; Exo. 32.13) and, finally, to the Nation of Israel (Lev. 20.24). It is a promise that will not fail of its final, intended fulfillment (2 Sam. 7.10; 1 Chron. 17.9).

[2]   E.g., Num. 27.11; 32.32; Deut. 2.31; 15.4; Judg. 2.6; 1 Chron. 28.8; etc.

One may enter into some place (e.g., my house), but not for the purpose of possessing it. Twelve men under the direction of Moses first entered the Land of Promise, not to possess it, but only to spy it out (Num. 13.16). Later, Joshua sent men into Jericho for the same reason (Josh. 6.25). Therefore, to simply enter into some place differs entirely from entering in to inherit and possess that place.

The Israelites were afflicted in Egypt for four hundred years (foretold in Gen. 15.13); but God ordained that they should exit Egypt, go to, enter, and take possession of the Promised Land; they were not called to enter the Land to become joint-citizens with its occupants.

There was, however, a danger under the Mosaic Covenant of disinheritance. In God's anger over the faithlessness and the disobediences of the first, adult generation of Israelites who had exited Egypt, He vowed, "I will strike them with the pestilence and disinherit them" (Num. 14.12). And indeed, that entire generation, excepting two,[3] perished during their wanderings in the wilderness over the next forty years. Nevertheless, God's earlier promise to the fathers did not fail of its fulfillment; for He brought the second generation of Israelites into the Land, where they eventually found rest.

Just as possessing and inheriting are very often conjoined in the O.T., likewise possession of and rest in that inheritance are frequently linked with one another.[4]

Inheritance of the Firstborn

There were significant benefits afforded to the firstborn males of ancient days. They were to have a threefold blessing over their brethren: blessings which were to be realized upon the death of their father.

---

[3] Joshua and Caleb: see Num. 14.22ff,28ff; Psa. 95.10f; Heb. 3.10f; 4.3b-5.
    It is of further interest to notice that Moses, Israel's leader, was disqualified from entering into the Land because of a certain sin committed against the LORD as described in Num. 20.8-12; 27.12-14.

[4] E.g., Deut. 3.20,21; 12.9,10; 25.19; Josh. 1.13-15; 22.4; 1 Chron. 22.17,18.

1. They were to be the head of their family

2. They were to be the priest of that family

3. They were to inherit a double portion of their father's wealth

Disqualified of Inheritance

Firstborn rights could and still can be lost.

The Nation of Israel was acknowledged by the LORD to be His son, His firstborn among the nations (Exo. 4.22); and the Nation owned the LORD as their Father.[5] But, as we have just discovered, the entire first generation of the Nation lost its right of inheritance. This same loss has been and can be the case even for individual, firstborn sons.

Esau, Isaac's eldest son, lost his firstborn birthright to his younger twin brother, Jacob, because the former one despised it (Gen. 25.34), trading it away for a meal of bread and lentil stew.

Reuben, Jacob's firstborn son, went into his father's concubine, Bilhah.[6] Therefore, when Jacob prophesied unto his sons, Reuben's right of rulership was granted to his brother, Judah (Gen. 49.8ff). God made the tribe of Levi (another of Reuben's brothers) to serve as priests and ministers unto the LORD in Israel (Num. 8.14ff). A double portion of the Land went to Reuben's brother, Joseph, posthumously, through Joseph's sons, Ephraim and Manasseh (Gen. 48.21f).

These examples are recorded for our benefit, in order that we may know that the abuse of grace is not without consequence.

Inheritance Under the New Covenant

Some additional background information will be helpful as we begin our present subsection.

---

[5] Exo. 4.22; Isa. 64.8.

[6] Gen. 35.22; 49.3,4.

The Jews of Jesus' day were awaiting the coming of Messiah as a mighty chieftain who would exalt their Nation above all the other nations. That their Deliverer would first appear as a meek and lowly Servant of men, One who came to save His people from their sins— this they did not understand; but they should have, according to their own Scriptures (John 5.39). Therefore, when Jesus Christ appeared as the Lamb of God they did not receive Him; for they presumed that the Law of Moses contained sufficient means to make atonement for their sins. The Jews expected a National Savior, not a Savior from sin. They were surely not ready to receive the Son of God: see John 5.18.

Some hold to differing definitions of the terms "kingdom of God" and "kingdom of heaven." Because these terms are often interchanged (see footnote 2, page 21), no distinction is being made in this writing. However, when either term appears in the N.T., it sometimes refers to a kingdom invisible and in other places to its manifest, future reality.

Paul says in Colossians that "[God] has delivered us *[past tense]* out from the authority of darkness and transferred *us* into the *[present, spiritual]* kingdom of His beloved Son" (Col. 1.13). We who are presently abiding in this spiritual kingdom should be patiently waiting for Jesus' appearing as the King in His manifest kingdom, and we are instructed to pray for that kingdom to come.[7]

Some few Jews believed that Jesus was their Messiah when he first came, and they thought that the appearing of His kingdom was imminent (Luke 19.11).[8] Therefore, Jesus informed them that a long delay would intervene their day and the day of His (second) coming in His kingdom in the Parables of the Talents (Matt. 25.19) and the Minas (Luke 19), and N.T. saints have ever lived in that delay.

In a careful examination of the N.T. it can be said with confidence that the kingdom has come (spiritually, in mystery), and is yet to come (in its glorious manifestation with the Lord Jesus as its King).

---

[7] Matt. 6.10; Luke 11.2; (1 Cor. 1.7; 2 Tim. 4.1).

[8] "They thought that the kingdom of God should immediately appear."

Let us now turn to the specific subject of inheritance under the New Covenant. Whenever we read of entering the kingdom to inherit it, it has reference to the Millennial kingdom; and this inheritance will be granted if our work of faith is adjudged to be worthy by Christ. Works, and not faith alone, is the issue of this inheritance.

Those who are adjudged as worthy of resurrection and/or rapture unto inheriting the Millennial kingdom will not enter it passively to be its mere citizens. Rather, they will enter it as co-heirs with Christ to possess it and to rule and reign together with Him (Rev. 2.26f; 3.21). Becoming co-heirs with Christ in His kingdom is the prize (the reward) of the high calling of God in Christ Jesus under the New Covenant.

Simply reclining in the good things of this life, afforded even to unbelievers, is not a gateway to inheritance of the Millennial kingdom.

The Out-resurrection

The discussion of resurrection and rapture in our previous chapter emphasized rapture. Here, I will say more about the specific matter of resurrection as it concerns our present subject of inheritance.

Paul gives an explanation to the Philippians of the reason why he gladly suffered the loss of all things as he pursued Christ. Please open your Bibles to Philippians, chapter three. His explanation is as follows.

> Phil. 3.4-14 …11 if by any means I may attain unto the resurrection from the dead.
> 12 Not that I have already obtained *it*, or am already made perfect; but I press on, if so be that I may lay hold of *that* for which I was also laid hold of by Christ Jesus. 13 Brethren, I do not consider myself to have laid hold *of it*. But one thing *I do*: forgetting indeed the things that are behind *me*, and straining forward to *the things* ahead *of me*, 14 I press on toward *the* goal for the prize of the high calling of God in Christ Jesus.[9]

---

[9] The italicized "*it*"s and "*that*" of verses 12 and 13 are rightly supplied by the translators and they all have reference to the same thing, as we shall soon see.

When reading your own version of the Bible you will see that Paul had forsaken all of the things that were of previous importance to him (Phil. 3.4-8) in order that he "might gain [or, win] Christ" (v. 8). By connecting the dots in verses 11-14, we can see that the "*it*"s and "*that*" (vv. 12,13), "the prize" (v. 14), and "the resurrection from the dead" (v. 11) are all one thing.

If resurrection unto eternal life is God's warrant to all who are in Christ—and it is (John 6.40,44)—why is Paul here referring to resurrection as something he was straining and pressing on to obtain? The following several points will lead us to the answer.

- The Jews in Jesus' day, and those throughout prior centuries, understood resurrection as a single, one-time event. Martha confessed to Jesus that she knew that her dead brother, Lazarus, would "rise again in the resurrection in the last day" (John 11.24).[10]

- But Jesus brought in a new revelation: that there would be "a resurrection from the dead." This was something new: a distinction between "resurrection of the dead" and "resurrection from the dead."

  "Resurrection from the dead" identifies a resurrection of some out from (Greek, *ek*) among the entire company of dead ones. In English, to say, "There were some prisoners who escaped out from among the prisoners in the prison" implies something different than to say, "The prisoners escaped from the prison."

  This "resurrection from the dead" was something that even Jesus' disciples did not understand early on.[11] But Paul, in his day, was active and aggressive, seeming to be obsessed with attaining unto this resurrection.

---

[10] In the Greek, the literal reading is, "in (*en*) the resurrection in (*en*) the last day."

[11] Mark 9.9f,31; Luke 9.44f; 18.31-34.

- "Resurrection" in the N.T. ordinarily derives from the Greek word *anastasis*. Here—and only here, in Phil. 3.11—"resurrection" is a translation of the Greek word *exanástasis*. This compound word, *exanástasis*, means "out-resurrection." In the Greek texts the entire phrase in which this word appears literally reads, "the out-resurrection out from *among* dead *ones*."

  The rendering, "resurrection of the dead" (in the KJV, MKJV, YLT, and Webster of Phil. 3.11), is incorrect and misleading; for all who are dead will not arise unto the *exanástasis*.

- This *exanástasis* is the special, exalted resurrection (the prize) which we hope to be found worthy of by Christ.

  Along with others, I believe this *exanástasis* is synonymous with "the first resurrection"—a superior one—mentioned in Rev. 20.5f: the resurrection that will result in certain of the saints reigning with Christ as His co-heirs in the Millennial kingdom.

  Concerning the prize of Phil. 3.14, we read in verse 12 that Paul was pressing on in order that he "may lay hold of *it*."[12] The urgency implied in his words does not bring to mind one who is passively reclining in the self-assurance of one day receiving something; for Paul was straining and pressing on to obtain and to lay hold of the prize (vv. 12ff)—"if by any means..." (v. 11).

"If by any means" he might obtain unto this resurrection. While resurrection, as such, was his warrant as God's gift, Paul foresaw the

---

[12] The Greek, *katalábōo*, rendered as "may lay hold of" (v. 12) is in the subjunctive mood; see footnote 1 on page 95. While Paul was pressing on to make this prize his reality, it was, at this earlier time, no more than potential. It was a time when he feared the possibility of being found disqualified of it in the end (1 Cor. 9.27); but he was later assured by the Lord that he would receive it (2 Tim. 4.8).

wondrous value of the out-resurrection: a resurrection to be gained as a reward for faithful service to the Master.

Paul not only strove to obtain this reward for himself; for he (and Timothy, and many others) labored in preaching, warning, and teaching all the saints "in order that [they] might present every man perfect *[complete, mature]* in Christ Jesus" (Col. 1.28). If one's work of faith and suffering for the gospel's sake will yield no distinctions in the end, the efforts of Paul and the others on behalf of the (already saved) saints were pointless—like beating the air (cp. 1 Cor. 9.26).

We Have Been Qualified

> Col. 1.12 …[the Father] has qualified us unto *[becoming]* the partaker of the inheritance….

The Holy Spirit is our Enabler, given to us by God's grace in order that we "might be filled with the full knowledge of His will in all wisdom and spiritual understanding…" (Col. 1.9ff);[13] for "His divine power has given to us *[once and for all]* all things that *pertain* to life and godliness" (2 Pet. 1.3).

Now this is a marvelous thing: that He has qualified[14] us to be the partaker[15] of the inheritance. Blessed be God for such a motivating hope.

However, as noted earlier, we must not ignore the gracious means made available to us in Christ; for this inheritance is conditional.

---

[13] That we "might be filled…"; for one may ignore the command of Eph. 5.18b.

[14] "Qualified" means "equipped; made sufficient, fit, and adequate." The Greek word, *hikanoósanti*, translated as "has qualified" ("made…meet," KJV) in this verse is in the aorist tense, meaning (here) that it occurred at some past point in time. In our case, that point in time was when the Spirit of Christ came to dwell within us upon our becoming God's children—His heirs (Rom. 8.16f)—through faith.

  "His divine power has given *[perfect, completed tense]* to us all things which *relate* to life and godliness" (2 Pet. 1.3). He has given us Christ.

[15] "Partaker" means "a sharer or participant; one who has a portion in something."

Chapter 15

Conditional Inheritance

All that God has sworn to do in His Word is guaranteed of its fulfill-ment. "I am God, and there is none like Me, declaring the end from the beginning, and from ancient times things which have not been done, saying, 'My purpose will be established, and I will accomplish all My good pleasure'" (Isa. 46.9f).[1] Baron has well written: "This is sure and certain, that however long the pause may last, God never loses the thread of the purpose which He has formed for this earth; and as surely as the prophecies of the sufferings of Christ have been fulfilled, so surely will those also be which relate to His glory and reign."[2]

However, and not withstanding this fact, God's promises, as they concern individuals, are often conditional—they are if/then kinds of propositions, even with respect to unbelievers. I will support this affir-mation below.

A Testament

One's last will and testament is a directive prepared according to the determined good pleasure of the testator. A testator has the right to

---

[1] God's oaths will be performed! (Gen. 26.3; Deut. 7.8; 2 Sam. 21.7; 1 Chron. 16.16; Psa. 105.9; Jer. 11.5; Dan. 9.11; Luke 1.72f; Acts 2.30; Heb. 6.17; 7.28)

[2] From *Zechariah: A Commentary on His Visions and Prophecies* by David Baron, published by Kregel Publishing; page 317.

make the benefits to be passed on to his heirs to be either guaranteed or conditional, or both.

For example: Mr. Jones may will that all of his living children are to receive an equal share of his estate upon his death. On the other hand, he may stipulate that none of his heirs will receive their portion unless and until they have fulfilled some stated condition—e.g., obtaining a college degree. Or, both may be combined in his final decree: a certain benefit being guaranteed to all of his heirs, while an additional benefit may be made conditional.

This last example is the case within our present consideration, where God is the Testator in Christ. Those who have been sealed with the Holy Spirit of promise presently possess the earnest (the down payment) of their inheritance of eternal life and the assurance of resurrection[3]—unconditionally.

However, there remains a portion of our inheritance—one of ruling and reigning with Christ—that is conditional. Paul makes these separate truths known in his epistle to the believers in Rome.

> Rom. 8.16,17 The Spirit Himself bears witness with our spirit that we are children of God. 17 And if children, then heirs—heirs of God [of His eternal life]; and joint-heirs with Christ if indeed we suffer together with *Him*, in order that we may also be glorified together *with Him*.

Herein, with respect to believers, we see Paul moving from an unconditional (and irrevocable) inheritance on to one conditional. Two heirships are in view in our present passage: [i] being heirs of God's eternal life because of our having been begotten of Him through faith in His Son; and [ii] the possibility of our becoming joint-heirs with Christ, "if indeed...."[4]

---

[3] John 3.36a; 6.40,44,54; Eph. 1.13f.

[4] "If indeed," here, is a subordinating (conditional) conjunction. Over the years I have been criticized by many—but without correction from Scripture—for subscribing to this view of two heirships. And if you, dear Christian, can come alongside of me in this persuasion, be prepared for this same criticism.

"If indeed..."

This second appearance of the word "if" in verse 17[5] finds considerable controversy among commentators and lexicologists. Some, who follow along with the opinion of M. R. Vincent in his *Word Studies*, may agree with him when he says, "Joint-heirs…If so be that (*eiper*) …assumes the fact. If so be, as is really [actually] the case."[6]

Others hold to a view recorded in Joseph H. Thayer's *Greek-English Lexicon*: "properly, *if on the whole; if only, provided that*, is used *of a thing which is assumed to be, but whether rightly or wrongly is left in doubt*" (italics are Thayer's). No one having read this far will be surprised to know that I subscribe without reservation to this latter proposition. I hold that this second "if" is to be understood as possible, but not guaranteed—i.e., if indeed, or if so be the case as stated—and I suspect that this would be the first and natural understanding of the vast majority of ordinary readers of the N.T. If Paul's statement in Rom. 8.17 is not intended to imply such a condition, he might just as well have written, "And if children, then heirs—heirs of God; and joint-heirs with Christ *because we are suffering* together with Him, *and we will therefore* also be glorified together with Him." I would wonder in amazement if anyone may assume that all believers are suffering together with Christ.

Decrees—Unconditional and Conditional

"Yes" and "Amen"—these are God's decrees, sealed in Him and certain of their fulfillment (2 Cor. 1.20). But as to how they pertain to any particular individual…this is a matter of a different kind. Only obedience of faith gives assurance to individuals of obtaining the conditional inheritance. The condition is, "having done the will of God" (Heb. 10.35f).

God's decrees, both conditional and unconditional, apply to all.

---

[5]   Rom. 8.17, where it reads "if indeed": *eiper* in the Greek texts.

[6]   Parenthesis is Vincent's; bracketed word is mine, only to enhance his meaning.

- Unbelievers. Men are beckoned by Jesus, "Come unto Me" to be saved. Though none are naturally willing to come, this will not annul God's intention to save men.[7]

- Unbelievers and believers. Whether one will be adjudged under the Law of sin and death (Rom. 8.2) or under the Law of Christ (Gal. 6.2) makes a distinction. But God's decree that every man will be judged according to his works is certain.[8]

- Believers. The word of the kingdom put forth to believers is no assurance that every one of them will receive it. Many who do receive it may give way under persecution and/or the cares of the world. Yet upon some this word will fall into the good ground of their heart; these are those who will diligently seek Him and bring forth fruit, albeit in differing degrees.[9] But the waywardness of individual believers will by no means negate God's determination that Jesus Christ will have worthy joint-heirs to rule and reign with Him.

Inheritance Through Obedience of Faith

Failure in Days of Old

The first mentions of inheritance in the Bible are found in Genesis, chapter 15. Therein, the LORD spoke to Abram (Abraham) as follows.

> Gen. 15.4-7 ...Then He said to him, "I am the LORD, who brought you out of Ur of the Chaldeans, to give you this Land to inherit it."

The Land-promise to Abraham was passed down through Isaac to Jacob and, eventually, to the Nation of Israel. As noticed earlier, the

---

[7] See Matt. 11.28ff; Mark 2.17; John 7.37f: then see Rom. 3.3,10ff.

[8] Matt. 16.27; Rom. 2.6; Rev. 2.23.

[9] See Jesus' explanation of the Parable of the Sower in Matt. 13.18-23.

first generation of the Nation was denied entrance into the Land because of unbelief and disobedience. However, God's determined purpose was not voided because of the failure of even an entire generation; it was, instead and indeed, accomplished when He brought in the next generation of Israelites. (Together, inheritance and heirship are referenced more than two-hundred and eighty times in the O.T.[10])

I will close out this brief subsection by noticing something that Paul asks rhetorically and answers emphatically in the N.T. "If some did not believe, will their unbelief nullify the faithfulness[11] of God *[to His Word]*? May it never be!" (Rom. 3.3).

The failures of old remain a possibility under the New Covenant.

Failure Under The New Covenant

Covenants were ratified by blood in the Bible. The New Covenant was ratified by the shedding of Messiah's blood.[12] This New Covenant is a better Covenant than the Mosaic one, and it is based on better promises. It is the bringing in[13] of a better hope (a heavenly hope); it is of a better and an abiding substance; it concerns a better resurrection.[14]

However, the New Covenant's betterness may fail of its intended end in the lives of God's children, even unto dire consequence. This is discovered in one of the sternest warnings to believers in the N.T.

> Heb. 10.28-31   Anyone who has rejected Moses' law
> dies without mercy on the testimony of two or three

---

[10] E.g., Gen. 15.4; Exo. 15.17; Num. 26.52f; Josh. 1.6; Jer. 49.2; Micah 1.15.

[11] Here, the correct rendering of the Greek word *pístis* is "faithfulness" and not "faith." "Faithfulness" is also the rendering from *pístis* in many translations of Matt. 23.23; Rom. 3.3; Gal. 5.22. Our Omniscient Father does not have faith; rather, He is faithful to His Word. See the definition of "faith" in Heb. 11.1.

[12] Cp. Gen. 15.9ff and Jer. 34.18f with Matt. 26.28 and Heb. 12.24.

[13] In Heb. 7.19, the Greek word *epeisagoge* is translated as "bringing in"; it means "a bringing in besides" (Thayer). Under the Mosaic Law, hope was earthly; under the New Covenant a hope of heavenly inheritance has been brought in.

[14] All of these affirmations are confirmed in Heb. 7.19,22; 8.6; 10.34; 11.35.

witnesses. 29 How much worse punishment, do you suppose, will be deserved by the one who has trampled the Son of God underfoot, counted the blood of the covenant by which he was sanctified *[saved]* a common thing, and insulted the Spirit of grace? 30 ..."The LORD will judge His people." 31 It is a fearful thing to fall into the hands of the living God.

A punishment worse than death?!

As noticed above, the promises of God with respect to a nation or an individual are most often of a provisional nature, their being if/then kinds of propositions. Let us test this affirmation by considering only a few excerpts from among many in the N.T. wherein this if/then principle may be discovered.[15]

> Matt. 5.5   Blessed are the meek: for they shall inherit the earth. *[If one is meek, then he shall inherit the earth.]*

> Matt. 19.29   And every one that hath forsaken houses, or brethren, or sisters, or father, or mother, or wife, or children, or lands, for my name's sake, shall receive an hundredfold, and shall inherit everlasting life. *[If one forsakes (lets go of) ordinary things in this life, then he shall inherit something better in the age to come: see Mark 10.28f.]*

> Gal. 5.19-21   Now the works of the flesh are evident, which are *[and then follows a list of them]*...those who practice such things will not inherit the kingdom of God. *[If one practices the works of the flesh, then he shall not inherit the kingdom: cp. 1 Cor. 6.9-10; Eph. 5.5.]*

> Heb. 6.12   ...be not slothful, but followers of them who through faith and patience are inheriting the promises. *[If one is a slothful believer, then he is not on his way to inheriting the promises.]*

> 1 Pet. 3.8,9   ...all of you be of one mind, having compassion for one another; love as brothers, be ten-

---

[15] While the words "if" and "then" are nearly always absent, the if/then principle is not invalidated; for it is obvious in the ordinary implication of language, as we shall see in the verses following.

derhearted, be courteous; 9 not returning evil for evil or reviling for reviling, but on the contrary blessing, knowing that you were called to this, in order that you may inherit a blessing. *[If a believer reciprocates evil with evil, or reviling for reviling, then he may not inherit a blessing.]*

Rev. 21.7   He who overcomes shall inherit all things, and I will be his God and he shall be My son. *[If a Christian overcomes, then....]*

For lack of space, other references are footnoted for the benefit of those eager to further verify for themselves that this conditional if/ then principle can be easily discovered in many N.T. declarations to believers.[16]

Let us now move along to learn more about the kingdom inheritance put before believers under God's New Covenant in Christ.

The Inheritance Set Before Us

This inheritance, as previously affirmed, has reference to the Millennial kingdom, a portion of which is being reserved for all those revealed to be of Christ in His presence (1 Cor. 15.23). They will be those begotten ones who have walked "worthy of God, who has called [us] into His kingdom and glory" (1 Thess. 2.12). To be numbered among the worthy is our "hope of His calling" (Eph. 1.18). This inheritance is the reward of Col. 3.24. It is the reward to be brought with Christ upon His return (Rev. 22.12).

Who among us can imagine the glory of such a thing?

Paul admonishes us through his words addressed to the Ephesian elders in Acts 20.31f: "Therefore, watch *[be on the alert]*, remembering that night and day for a period of three years I did not cease to admonish each one with tears. And now, brethren, I commend you to

---

[16]   Matt. 5.20,29,30; 6.14,15; 18.3,34,35; Luke 16.11,12; Rom. 8.16,17; 14.3,4; 1 Cor. 3.12-15; 9.17a; Col. 1.21-23; 2 Tim. 2.5,11,12; Heb. 2.2,3a; 3.14,15; 6.3; 10.38; 12.14,25; 1 John 3.20,21; Rev. 3.3,20; 22.18,19.

God and to the word of His grace, which is able to build you up and to give you the inheritance among all those who have been sanctified."[17]

Would Paul, for three years, "admonish" (warn; Greek, *noutheteo*) these same ones—ones who were born-again "brethren"—concerning this inheritance unless there was a possibility of their coming short of obtaining it?[18]

To his (saved) disciple, Titus, Paul writes that "having been justified by His grace, we might become heirs according to hope of eternal life" (Titus 3.7).[19] Eternal life is the warrant of God upon faith unto all who believe—we have been justified. But our hope of eternal life is something else. It is a hope of an abundant entrance into Christ's kingdom. This hope looks forward to our being "accounted worthy to attain unto that age *[the Millennial Age]* and to the resurrection out from among *the* dead *ones*"—(this is a more literal rendering of Luke 20.35).

Near the end of his life, the apostle Paul—having earlier stated that he had not yet been perfected or obtained the prize (Phil. 3.12ff)—wrote the following to his disciple, Timothy.

> 2 Tim. 4.7,8   I have fought the good fight, I have finished the course, I have kept the faith. 8 In the future there is laid up for me the crown of righteousness, which the Lord, the righteous Judge, will award to me in that Day; and not only to me, but also to all those loving His appearing.

---

[17] Barnes, in his *Notes* under Acts 20.32, writes as follows: "They who receive a part in the inheritance beyond the grave will have it only among the sanctified and the pure. They must, therefore, be pure themselves, or they can have no part in the kingdom of Christ and of God."

In 2 Cor. 7.1, we are instructed to be "perfecting holiness in the fear of God." Personally knowing (being exercised in) the fear of the Lord, we ought to always be submitting ourselves to Christ's activity within us.

[18] 2 Cor. 6.1; Heb. 4.1; 12.15ff.

[19] The phrase "having been justified" in Titus 3.7 is in the aorist tense: here, a past occurrence. However, the phrase "we might become heirs" is in the subjunctive mood (see footnote 1 on page 95), denoting something that can and might well become reality, though the fact is left in question.

I offer the following two thoughts in light of this passage from Second Timothy. First, "that Day" is the Day of Christ's presence (His *parousia*). While still ministering, Paul's eager desire was not to die—to be unclothed (i.e., without a covering, a body)—but to be clothed with a habitation which is from heaven, in order that being so clothed he should not be found naked. I understand this clothing to be a resurrection body to be received in the day of our redemption.[20]

Secondly, Paul stresses that reward necessitates "loving His appearing." But how many believers think daily (or monthly, or yearly) about His appearing, let alone loving and longing for it? Many have never even received the message of the kingdom as a little child.[21] Others have only this occasional thought: that when they die they will go to heaven as a naked soul—and this despite what may be their present, wayward manner of living. Even now, some of these same errant ones may say that they are expecting to be raptured at any moment. Oh my!

A young woman's husband may need to leave her for a time to attend to certain, specific matters concerning his father's business. And if his wife may truly love him, will she not be longing continually for his reappearance, keeping his house fit for his return?

Hypocrisy in a Christian's Life

Men abhor hypocrisy; so does our Lord (Matt. 23.13ff).

Dearly beloved: Christians cannot show up at the church-house with their Sunday go-to-meeting teeth on, patting the saints on the back with a "Bless you," and thereafter go home to subject their wives to unloving, even vile speech; or to nag their husbands; or to exasperate their children with angry disciplines too severe. Neither can they be known to be living in some moral fault; for any/all such bad behavior will invalidate any witness for Christ to others, leaving unbelievers to

---

[20] This matter is addressed in Rom. 8.23; 1 Cor. 15.35ff; 2 Cor. 5.2-4.

[21] Mark 10.15; Luke 18.17.

wonder: "How is it possible that God would condemn me but not these who call themselves Christians?—for I deem myself to be leading a better life than many of them." Is it any surprise that so many unbelievers often dismiss interest in the necessity of Christ's salvation based on the hypocrisy to be observed in the lives of certain Christians?

> 1 John 3.2,3   Beloved, now we are children of God, and what we shall be has not yet been manifested; *but* we know that whenever He shall be manifested, we will be like Him, because we will see Him as He is. 3 And everyone having this hope *set* on Him purifies himself, even as He is pure.

Hope and purity of life are interdependently related.

Hypocrisy is an obstacle to influencing men unto faith in Christ; purity in life and character will give weight to our testimony. The writer of Hebrews says, "[God] spoke long ago to the fathers in the prophets…in these last days *He* has spoken to us in His Son" (Heb. 1.1,2). "In"—namely, in and through their lives. Simple words alone will not frequently persuade others; it is in a man's observable manner of life that he speaks loudest.

> Heb. 4.1 Let us therefore fear, lest a *[conditional]* promise being left to us of entering into His rest, any of you should seem to come short of it.

Chapter 16

Overcoming

"To him who overcomes…" (Revelation 2-3)

Precious Promises

In Revelation, chapters 2 and 3, we find a record of seven letters dictated by our glorified Lord to John, the Revelator. While they were separately addressed to each of seven churches, they were intended to be shared among all. These letters contain Christ's assessment of each church. Within six of the churches He notices certain things approved of; to five He expresses some displeasure. Yet all are encouraged in one way or another; and all who will overcome are given specific promises.

Here is a summary of Christ's promises "to him who overcomes."

- He will be privileged to eat of the Tree of Life, which is in the midst of the Paradise of God (2.7).

- He shall not be hurt of the Second Death (2.11).[1]

- He will eat of the hidden manna, and he will receive a white stone with a new name written in the stone which no man knows but he who receives it (2.17).

---

[1] If overcomers "shall not be hurt of the Second Death," what does this suggest concerning lazy, wicked, non-overcoming Christians?

- He will have power over the nations; and he shall receive the Morning Star (2.26-28).[2]

- He will be clothed in white raiment; his name will not to be blotted out of the Book of Life, but confessed by Christ before His Father and before His angels (3.5).

- He will be made a pillar in the temple of His God; the name of His God, and His new name, and the name of the city of His God—which is New Jerusalem—will be written upon him (3.12).

- He will sit with Christ in His throne (3.21).

These promises pertain to overcomers and—if the plain and simple implications of language mean anything—it is obvious that the believer who does not overcome will not be a partaker of these promises of our glorified Lord.

Intimacy with Christ

During the period of Jesus' earthly ministry, men experienced differing degrees of acquaintance, camaraderie, and intimacy with Him.

There were multitudes that followed after Him and addressed Him as "Lord"; but sadly, many had various excuses for leaving off.[3]

Of those who continued with Him, seventy were separated out and sent to preach the gospel of the kingdom and to demonstrate that the kingdom of God had come near unto the people (Luke 10).

There were twelve chosen to enjoy more fraternity with the Master than did others. From among those twelve disciples there were four, then three, and finally one (John) who enjoyed increasing degrees of privilege and intimacy with Jesus.[4]

---

[2]   Cp. Rev. 2.28 with 22.16. This "Morning Star" is Christ in His kingdom.

[3]   Luke 9.57-62; John 6.60,66.

[4]   Mark 5.37ff; 13.3ff; 14.32f; Luke 9.28ff; John 13.23,25; 19.26f; 21.20ff.

Many of the begotten have not sought out the narrow way that leads to life; some do seek this way and will enter into the joy of the Lord in His Millennial reign. In that Age, He will configure their associations with Himself just as He did during His first days upon the earth.

Failure Through Indifference

Despite the glory of it all, I have heard believers say words like these: "Well, at least I have eternal life, and that's enough for me. I'm not interested in a reward, or in ruling or reigning with Christ. I'm grateful just to know that I'm saved."

I must confess that this was my own private prayer of praise and thanksgiving years ago. However, I have since come to see that this is careless speech; it demonstrates a certain indifference concerning the glorious inheritance set before every Christian. Such indifference reminds us of Esau, who despised his birthright and sold it to his brother, Jacob, for a morsel of food.[5] But on the day that their father, Isaac, actually awarded the birthright to Jacob—the supplanter—Esau was reduced to crying out "with an exceedingly great and bitter cry." Nevertheless, his father would not change his mind in the matter.[6] Likewise, no tears or bitter crying will reverse Christ's righteous decrees when believers appear before His judgment seat.

Esau was an earthy man, drawn away by the lusts of the flesh, having no interest to his firstborn rights. Paul warns believers that they may be beguiled and drawn aside or away by other interests, even of a spiritual kind,[7] their minds being "corrupted from the simplicity that is in Christ" (2 Cor. 11.3).

May none of us become indifferent in this matter. Instead, let us press on in order that we might not see our inheritance forfeited,

---

[5] Gen. 25.29-34; Heb. 12.16.

[6] Gen. 27.34; Heb. 12.17.

[7] See Col. 2.18 with respect to false spirituality.

thereby missing out on that special, personal communion with our Lord in His Millennial reign. Let us not fall short and fail to overcome.[8]

Pray, beloved, that this latter end will not be our case.

Hindrances to Overcoming

There are hindrances that continually afflict the lives and the faith of believers, and they may bring about the disqualification of those who have been (originally) qualified to be overcomers.

There is Satan and his minions. We are instructed to "resist the devil" (Jas. 4.7). Satan's nature and activities are as follows.

- Satan is a deceiver, a liar, and the father of lies.[9]

- He was a murderer from the beginning; he comes only "to steal, and to kill, and to destroy."[10]

- He is the evil one who snatches away the word of the kingdom, heard by men and sown in their hearts, lest they should believe it.[11]

- He is our adversary, the one who "walks about as a roaring lion, seeking whom he may devour" (1 Pet. 5.8).

Then, there is the world (and its ways) and our flesh; these interact to wage war against our soul. Concerning their activities, those who would overcome are admonished by Christ's apostles as follows.

- "Beloved, I urge you as foreigners and sojourners [in this world] to abstain from fleshly lusts which wage war against the soul"…"for our citizenship is in heaven."[12]

---

[8]   Rom. 12.21; Heb. 4.1; 12.15a; 2 Pet. 2.18ff.

[9]   (Gen. 3.13); John 8.44; 2 Cor. 11.3; 1 Tim. 2.14.

[10]   John 8.44; 10.10.

[11]   Matt. 13.19; Mark 4.15; Luke 8.12.

[12]   See 1 Pet. 2.11…Phil. 3.20. (In human society, citizenship may be revoked.)

- "Beware—lest any man carry you off through philosophy and empty deceit, after the tradition of men, after the rudiments of the world, and not after Christ" (Col. 2.8).

- "Love not the world, neither the things that are in the world. If anyone loves the world, the love of the Father is not in him.

    "For everything that is in the world—the lust of the flesh, and the lust of the eyes, and the pride of life—is not of the Father; it is of the world" (1 John 2.15f).

How May We Overcome?

The simple answer is, "We cannot; but Christ in us can."[13]

Many believers have become beguiled by things untrue.[14] They have become too entrenched in this world while neglecting meditation upon God's word, and prayer. Spiritual laziness, which leads to disobedience and unfaithfulness, is overcoming them.

However, among them are some who will willingly confess, "Yes, this is my case, and my soul is not at rest. Oh, how I wish to become an overcomer!"

I admit that this has been my own circumstance and confession from time to time during my Christian life. I pray that if it is presently yours, beloved, you may arise to overcome; for the means are even now at hand.

Jesus has "overcome the world" (John 16.33). He did so by fulfilling and accomplishing all the Law of God—both in spirit and in

---

[13] "With men this is impossible; but with God all things are possible." This statement by Christ, in its context, concerns the issue of inheritance (Matt. 19.26).

[14] A believer whose spiritual understanding and world view are in opposition to Scripture has been caught in the devil's snare (2 Tim. 2.24ff). We must do all that we can, in meekness and gentleness, to instruct them according to Christ.

conduct—as He gladly submitted His will to that of the Father who was dwelling in Him.[15] This was the way of life that led Jesus to being found worthy of glorification upon His ascension.

Likewise, we may overcome the world if we will lay hold of this unfathomable truth: "Christ, in [us], the hope of glory" (Col. 1.27)—i.e., our hope of glory is Christ working in and through us.

As the Father was in Christ, even so Christ is in us—in you. Jesus promised that the Holy Spirit, who was in Christ when He was with His disciples, would be in them (and us) after His resurrection.[16]

The Holy Spirit is our *Parakletos*—our Helper, Comforter, and Defender[17]—the One who will keep us and guide us into all truth (John 16.13) if we will not resist Him. This is marvelous to consider; it is something to encourage us and shore us up in times of despair.

We, like our Savior—though we are but dust (Psa. 103.14)—can overcome the world by seeking first (above all else) the kingdom of God and His righteousness (Matt. 6.33) as we continue to look upon Jesus and the joy that is set before us.

> Heb. 12.1-3 …Let us run with endurance the race that is set before us, 2 looking unto Jesus, the author and finisher of our faith, who, for the joy that was set before Him, endured the cross, despising the shame, and has sat down at the right hand of the throne of God.
>
> 3 For consider Him who endured such hostility from sinners against Himself, lest you become weary and discouraged in your souls.

A man who is fully, naturally equipped by God to become an Olympic champion swimmer may have no interest in the Games. He may have no interest in its prize or any desire to involve himself in the

---

[15] Matt. 5.17f; John 5.17,19,30; 6.38; 8.16,28f; 12.49,50; 14.10f; 16.33.

[16] John 14.17; 20.22; Acts 1.4f.

[17] The Greek word *parakletos* also appears in John 14.16,18; 14.26; 15.26; 16.7.

rigors required to obtain it;[18] his only interest may be recreational swimming. Therefore, this golden opportunity is forever lost to him.

However, I pray that you who have been qualified (equipped) to attain unto the reward of Christ—being motivated by having seen (in God's Word and in your spirit) its supreme value—will allow Christ to work in you unto its obtaining.

Addendum

> Matt. 16.24-27   Then Jesus said to His disciples, "If anyone desires to come after Me, let him deny himself, and take up his cross, and follow Me. 25 For whoever desires to save his *soul*-life will lose it, but whoever loses his *soul*-life for My sake will find it. 26 For what profit is it to a man if he gains the whole world, and loses his own soul? Or what will a man give in exchange for his soul? 27 For the Son of Man will come in the glory of His Father with His angels, and then He will reward each according to his works."

Well after having initially written this chapter many months ago, I ran across a book by Watchman Nee wherein he comments as follows on this passage from Matthew's gospel.

> This is what the Lord means: that all who are gratified by the world today shall lose the position of reigning with Him in the future. Consequently, the salvation of the soul is quite different from what we commonly know as the salvation of the spirit (which means having eternal life)....
>
> ...The passage which we have been considering tells us that if we lose our soul for the Lord's sake, our soul shall be saved. And hence the salvation of the spirit is to have eternal life while the salvation of the soul is to possess [inherit] the kingdom.

---

[18] To be equipped to obtain is no guarantee of obtaining.

> The spirit is saved through Christ bearing the cross
> for me; the soul is saved by my bearing a cross myself.[19]

Nee's words pertain exactly to my thesis concerning our being glorified together with Christ.

What should preoccupy us as believers is not the salvation of our spirit: that has been accomplished once and for all time. What ought to occupy all of our attention is the salvation of our soul,[20] through the resurrection life of Christ indwelling us, as we add to our faith the virtues mentioned in 2 Pet. 1.5ff, which were discussed on pages 100ff.

Dodson, with reference to Gal. 4.19, rightly notes: "Now [Paul] was 'travailing in birth *again* for them, that Christ might be formed in them.'"[21] Notice that Paul says "formed in," not "born again."

I pray, beloved, that we may all come to see the glory of Christ and His kingdom as more valuable than anything in this world.

Humble meditation upon the Word of God can bring our seeing and our desire for this precious experience into being, according as the indwelling Helper teaches, enables, warns, and comforts each of us.[22] We can overcome in the same manner as did the apostle Paul as we learn to live by faith of the Son of God: see Gal. 2.20.[23]

---

[19] From *The Salvation of the Soul: Part One*; published by Christian Fellowship Publishing, Inc.; p. 15; public domain website. Bracketed word is my inclusion.

Watchman Nee became a Christian in mainland China at the age of seventeen in 1920. Beginning in that same year, and for thirty-two years thereafter, he wrote and ministered. He was then cast into prison and severely persecuted for his faith by the Communist Chinese in 1952, dying in prison twenty years later. His writings are numerous, very precious, and easily obtained.

I like something else that Nee says in *The King and the Kingdom of Heaven*, published by Christian Fellowship Publishers, Inc.; p. 340—"To get people saved is a means, not an end."

[20] See also Psa. 35.9; 62.1; Isa. 61.10; Heb. 10.39; 1 Pet. 1.9; Jas. 1.21.

[21] From *The Prize of the Up-Calling* by Kenneth F. Dodson; published by Schoettle; p.135. "[Paul]" replaces "he" for identification; italic is Dodson's.

[22] John 14.26; 2 Cor. 1.3f; 5.10.

[23] Paul's words therein may mean "...faithfulness *[pistis]* of the Son of God...."

We shall become overcomers as we unrelentingly petition God for help, in prayer, confessing our sins, and surrendering our will and our ways to Him through Christ.

> Jer. 29.11 "For I know the thoughts that I think for you," declares the LORD, "thoughts of peace and not of calamity, to give you a future and a hope."

Chapter 17

Neglect Not So Great A Salvation

Promises and Admonitions

The N.T. is filled with promises and admonitions to help us remain spiritually awake and watchful in faith. As we eagerly await the coming of the Lord (His promise),[1] we are admonished to "work out [our] own salvation with fear and trembling,"[2] perfecting holiness in love and good works[3] unto the enduring of all things.[4] Let us not, dear saints, become wearied unto neglecting "so great a salvation" (Heb. 2.3).[5]

May the Lord help us to walk worthy of Him, pleasing Him, and being fruitful in every good work (Col. 1.10).

Warnings!

The Israelites of old exclaimed with great self-confidence: "All that the LORD has spoken we will do, and we will be obedient!" (Exo. 24.7).

---

[1] See Matt. 13.37; 24.44; Mark 13.35ff; Luke 12.40; Rom. 8.23,25; 13.11ff; Eph. 5.14ff; 1 Cor. 1.17b; Titus 2.13; Heb. 9.28; Rev. 16.15.

[2] Phil. 2.12 (cp. 1 Tim. 4.16).

[3] Matt. 5.16; John 13.34; 15.12,17; Rom. 6.19,22; 13.8; 2 Cor. 7.1; Eph. 2.10; 1 Thess. 3.13; 4.7; 1 Tim. 6.18; Titus 2.7; 3.8,14; Heb. 10.24; 1 Pet. 1.22.

[4] Mark 13.13; 1 Cor. 13.7; 2 Tim. 4.5; Jas. 1.12.

[5] This "so great a salvation" pertains to "holy brethren, partakers of the heavenly calling" (3.1); it is not referring to the initial salvation of unbelievers.

Nevertheless, not many days thereafter they were rejoicing before a golden calf idol (Exodus 32). The ultimate failure of human nature is discovered in every man—be he a Jew, a Gentile, or even a Christian.

A Christian may begin well, walking in the Spirit, only to later allow the world, the flesh, and the wiles (schemes) of the devil to get the better of him.

We may shudder as we read, with wonder and solemn attention, the following, frightful narrative recorded in Scripture for our sakes; for it certainly refers to what may become the terrible consequences for some wayward, willfully disobedient born-again ones.[6]

> Luke 12.42-48   And the Lord said *[to His disciples, vv. 22,41]*, "Who then is that faithful and wise steward, whom the Lord will put over His household, to give *them* a portion of food in due season? 43 Blessed *is* that servant whom his Lord will find so doing when he comes. 44 Truly, I say to you that He will make him ruler over all that He has.
>
> 45 "But if that servant says in his heart, 'My Lord is delaying His coming,' and begins to beat the male and female servants, and to eat and drink and be drunk, 46 the Lord of that servant will come on a day when he is not looking for Him, and at an hour when he is not aware, and will cut him in two and appoint him his portion with the unbelievers. 47 And that servant who knew his Lord's will, and did not prepare himself or do according to His will, shall be beaten with many stripes. 48 But he who did not know, yet committed things deserving of stripes, shall *[nevertheless]* be beaten with few *stripes.*"[7]

---

[6] "Willfully disobedient," when they well know better from God's Word.

[7] Some may suggest that the consequences noticed herein have reference to entering the Tribulation with unbelievers, and that those unfaithful servants will miss out on the rapture: the one to occur in an unexpected hour (cp. v. 46 above with Luke 12.40). Others may suggest that they have to do with being appointed a portion (but only a portion) with the "goats" noticed in Matt. 25.32ff. Whatever…they are things most awful to consider.

Two things are particularly noteworthy in our present passage. First, it is "that *[same]* steward"[8] who is at first identified as faithful, wise, and blessed, but who is subsequently found to have become the utter opposite.

Secondly, such a backslidden servant will be appointed "his portion with the unbelievers," be "beaten with many stripes" and "cut in two." These things, horrific to consider, may await some Christians—though, again, I would aver that such severities will be intended as disciplinary and temporal, and not vengeful or eternal.

Many other warnings appear in the N.T.; and though they are veiled in metaphor, they are surely dreadful. A list of some of them would include warnings to believers about being cast into gehenna[9] or into outer darkness;[10] being handed over to the torturers;[11] being rejected, burned, and near unto a curse;[12] facing God's fiery indignation (Heb. 10.27); etc. These consequences—the bad things of 2 Cor. 5.10 —are in addition to the forfeiture of kingdom inheritance.

The warnings above require no elaboration. However, in noticing how the N.T. writers encourage, instruct, and admonish all of us in the faith in so many other places, let us press on and persevere in patience, unto holiness, through the Lord's precious provision of His Holy Spirit, as we eagerly await the return of our great God and Savior Jesus Christ (Titus 2.13).

---

8   This "steward" is a "servant" (see vv. 43ff), a slave (Greek, *doulos*); and he represents one who is owned of God—viz., a Christian.

9   Matt. 5.22,29,30; 10.28; 18.9; Mark 9.43,45,47; Luke 12.5.

10   Matt. 8.10-12.

11   Matt. 18.21-35.

12   I would be totally mystified if the ones being referenced in Heb. 6.4-8 are not Christians. And while the gift of eternal life is irrevocable, this being burned— whatever it may mean and however terrible its experience may be—must have believers in view. Though I have defended the position that no believer will find his eternal abode in the Lake of Fire, I pray that the warnings noted above may be of great concern to any unrepentant, wayward Christian; for none of them are idle threats.

Closing Encouragements

While I am under obligation, according to the whole counsel of God, to have included the above warnings, I will close on this higher note.

Paul has given us great assurance and encouragement unto faithfulness when he writes: "Eye has not seen, nor ear heard, nor has *the* heart of man imagined the things which God has prepared for those who love Him" (1 Cor. 2.9).

Whatsoever things you and I may have imagined pertaining to the glory that God is calling us into, they are as nothing—for that glory exceeds every human notion.

If you, beloved of God, have fallen back, begin today to call upon Jesus for help. If you have a broken spirit and a broken and contrite heart, He will not despise you.[13] Take this from Scripture—and from one who knows first-hand of God's gracious and merciful deliverance on multiplied occasions since having been saved years ago.

---

[13] Psa. 51.17; 102.17.

Conclusion

Perhaps you have now experienced paradigm shift[1] in your faith. For too long, most Christians have only considered God's salvation as an act of His love—which it indeed is—without any understanding of His eternal purpose in saving sinners. He intends to glorify Himself in Christ and in all the faithful who will surrender their lives to Him.[2]

Even Christ's earliest disciples did not initially understand this, and many of your questions may remain unanswered. Many of them were, and some still continue to be my own; for "we know in part" (1 Cor. 13.9). In this writing, I have made every effort to rightly divide the Word of God and to stir you up. Others are left to fill in the blanks.

Let each reader be assured of one thing. I do not consider myself to have yet laid hold of the prize. Having written as I have, I am regularly concerned that I may not be found disqualified of Christ's reward. Fear and trembling have been my frequent companions during the past two decades. I have tried not to be "wise in my own opinion" (Rom. 12.16) while writing for your sakes as well as my own.

The truths of God's Word will be of no real profit to any of us if they only take up residence in our intellect; they must sink deep down into our heart in order to bring forth good fruit in our everyday life. I pray that this writing has not only informed you, but that it will lead to the transformation of your life and your hope.

---

[1] "Paradigm shift"—"a radical alteration in one's underlying belief system."

[2] John 13.31f; Eph. 2.7; 2 Thess. 1.10ff; 1 Pet. 4.11.

One May Wonder...

"Why has this message about conditional inheritance never been presented in our local assembly?" The answers to this question seem almost obvious.

1. The pastor or teacher may be unaware of this doctrine. If this is the case, it will likely be laid to his charge; for such instructors are responsible to see the deeper truths of Scripture, and to teach them to the saints in order that they may be perfected (matured): see Eph. 4.11ff.

2. Such teaching—if understood and taught by a pastor or teacher in the local assembly—would doubtless tend to emptying out the church-house. Will God-appointed messengers allow this—notwithstanding the fact that Jesus has informed us that His flock is a little one (Luke 12.23)?

But you, beloved, having read to the conclusion of this writing, ought not to be numbered among so many others; for you have heard of the wonderful inheritance set before all of us as a reward for faithful service to the Master. However, it has been my experience that of the many with whom I have shared this truth, most have not had an ear to hear it. Some thoughts concerning such neglectful hearing are these.

*   Many are satisfied with eating the loaves and being filled (cp. John 6.26); they are content as heirs of God's eternal life, delighting only and ever in listening repeatedly to messages of a blissful life in eternity.

*   Many resist hearing any teaching that puts forth the truth of the strictness of Christ's judgment with respect to believers. They protest: "He will surely not recompense any believer with things bad!"

*   Satan is better instructed in God's Word than we are. His ploy has been to beguile Christians into not believ-

ing all that God has said, leaving them to be selective hearers of His Word but not doers of it (Jas. 1.22).

- Lax Christians will not hear the whole counsel of God. They remain babes (Heb. 5.12ff), thereby delaying the overthrow of Satan;[3] this is Satan's unabated intention.

Since before the beginning of this age, Satan[4] has tried to thwart God's purposes. He is a beguiler—a great deceiver. Eve was the first to succumb to his deceptions in the Garden of Eden (Gen. 3.1ff). Satan's ways have not changed since before the creation of man; but he will meet his end, and his purposes will come to naught.

The eternal purposes of God, determined in Him from before anything was ever created, have been these.

- "...That in all things God may be glorified through Jesus Christ; to Him the glory and the dominion belongs forever and ever. Amen" (1 Pet. 4.11).

- That in the Millennial age, Jesus Christ will reign with His glorified co-heirs—resurrected and/or raptured believers who were joined in His sufferings (Rom. 8.17)

- "That in the ages to come, He might show the exceeding riches of His grace in *His* kindness toward us in Christ Jesus" (Eph. 2.7)

If this writing has awakened you to a glorious hope in Christ, and if these truths will effect a positive change for the better in how and by what means you will live out your Christian life from here on, then my labor has not been in vain. And because you have read to this end, I am persuaded of these better things concerning you, beloved.

Be not deceived along your way.

---

[3] See Mark 4.15,26-29; Rev. 14.14-16; 20.1-3.

[4] Previously, Lucifer ("the *[then]* morning star"; Isa. 14.12), who rebelled against God and is now called "Satan," meaning our "adversary."

Insertion

I am inserting some brief remarks by Hudson Taylor—remarks that I discovered well after having written an early draft of this book. They are in full agreement with my thesis. Godly Taylor wrote:

> We wish to place on record our solemn conviction that not all who are Christians, or think themselves such, will attain to that resurrection of which St. Paul speaks in Philippians 3:11, or will thus meet the Lord in the air. Unto those who by lives of consecration manifest that they are not of the world, but are looking for Him, "He will appear without sin unto salvation."[5]

Closing Thoughts

I would say this to every reader, but especially to the youngest ones. The terrible troubles to arise at the end of this age—troubles that may have begun by the time of your reading this book—will require your extraordinary faith and vision in order that you may overcome. "Where there is no vision, the people perish [or, cast off restraint]" (Prov. 29.18). But by now, beloved, you should have a clear vision of God's wondrous high calling unto the reward of the inheritance.

My heart throughout this writing is the same as another's: "It is hoped that, by the grace of the blessed Spirit of truth, these pages may give light to the open eye, food to the hungry soul, vigor to the spirit, courage to the dispirited, warning to the self-confident."[6]

As mentioned in the Preface, I pray that you have come to the end of this writing a changed person. Amen.

---

[5] These closing words from the Appendix of *Union and Communion* by Hudson Taylor—the world renowned Christian missionary to China—can be found on the following public domain e-book site: <http://ebookbrowse.com/union-and-communion-hudson-taylor-book-pdf-d191313317>; p. 27 of that PDF.

[6] From *The Revelation of Jesus Christ* by G. H. Lang, published by Schoettle Publishing Co., Inc.; p. 15.

Appendices

Concerning Objections to My Views on Death and Glory

Even in light of the supportive citations included in Chapter 7—which refute the notion that the soul of any departed believer has ascended directly into heaven's glory upon death—certain objections will still arise among believers. I will address three of the weightier ones in what follows.

2 Corinthians 12

An interpretive problem arises in 2 Cor. 12.1-4—one which has contributed to erroneous teaching within Christendom. Paul is therein writing about visions and revelations (plural) of the Lord (v. 1). He says that he knew a man (most obviously himself) who was "caught up to *[or,* even unto*]* a third heaven" (v. 2), and who was additionally (separately) "caught up into Paradise" (v. 4). But because the Greek word *harpazo* is rendered as "caught up" in nearly every English translation of verse 4, it is assumed by many that Paul was taken upward on both occasions. I must respectfully disagree.

The basic meaning of the Greek word *harpazo* (despite its rendering as "caught up" in 2 Cor. 12.4) mandates no specific direction of up, down, or sideways—except when its direction can be surely determined, in context, to be upward.

Three express examples of the upward meaning of *harpazo* are found in the N.T. First, in 2 Cor. 12.2, where Paul was "caught up unto a third heaven." Next, in 1 Thess. 4.17, where the saints are foretold of being "caught up in clouds" above the earth. Finally, the man child is seen to be "caught up unto God" in Rev. 12.5.

Aside from these examples, *harpazo*—in ten other occurrences in the Greek text—means "to snatch (away)" or "to catch (off),"[1] or "to take by force."[2] There is, therefore, no definitional requirement for our understanding that Paul was "caught up into Paradise" (v. 4), unless one presupposes this to be the location of the Paradise to which he is referring. "Caught away into *[the lower]* Paradise" is the better understanding.

Ephesians 4

One may ask: "Doesn't Paul say in Eph. 4.8, 'When [Christ] ascended on high, He led captivity captive?'" And while I answer, "Indeed it does!" it will require more than one verse to establish any doctrine.

A majority of believers assume that when Christ ascended into heaven, He emptied the lower Paradise of all of its disembodied, naked, captive souls, and that they now abide in God's heavenly Paradise above. They then go on to speculate that since that day the departed souls of all believers have ascended directly up unto heaven.[3] However, I believe that Eph. 4.8 can be more rightly understood as follows.

Jesus is "the firstborn out from the dead" (Col. 1.18). His companions will likewise come out from the dead through resurrection. Even for Jesus, bodily resurrection was a thing requisite to His ascension.

Prior to Christ's death and resurrection, men were held in bondage by the fear of death. The writer of Hebrews informs us that Christ came and died in order that "through death He might render powerless

---

[1]   Matt. 12.29; 13.19; John 10.12,28,29; Acts 8.39; Jude 23.

[2]   Matt. 11.12; John 6.15; Acts 23.10.

[3]   Anyone who furthermore suggests that these departed souls have received a resurrection body is proved to be a false witness based upon 2 Tim. 2.18.

the *one* having the power of death, that is, the devil; and that He might free those who through fear of death *[thereby being held captive by fear of its power]* were subject to bondage all their lives" (Heb. 2.14f).

Christians should be presently enjoying a spiritual peace concerning death, anticipating their final deliverance from it through resurrection. Jesus possesses "the keys of Death and Hades" (Rev. 1.18); and because He lives, believers, who presently possess eternal life, will live also (in bodily resurrection: future tense, John 5.28f).

In the Greek text of our present verse (Eph. 4.8) it is not "captives" (plural) who were led captive, but "captivity" (singular). This captivity—the fear of death—was taken captive by Christ, and it was led away with Him when He was raised from the dead, after which resurrection He appeared to many eyewitnesses. Jesus preached "deliverance to the captives" (Luke 4.18); He has assured us that "the gates of Hades shall not *[future tense]* prevail against [the Church]" (Matt. 16.18).

If one will reject this view on the basis of Matt. 27.52f[4]—saying that those who arose from the dead after Christ's resurrection initiated the captivity led captive—I would notice that [i] the many resurrected saints (for not all were resurrected) had obviously been accounted as worthy of such a resurrection, but the Bible is silent as to what became of them thereafter; and [ii] with respect to Enoch and Elijah—types in the O.T. of those who will experience rapture—the Bible is also silent concerning whatever ultimately became of them.

The conjectures of men should not usurp Biblical silence.

Finally, let us once more recall something that the apostle John recorded years after Jesus' ascension:[5] "No one has ascended into heaven except He who came down from heaven, *even* the Son of Man *who is in the heaven*" (John 3.13).

---

[4] Matthew 27.52,53: "And the graves were opened; and many bodies of the saints which slept arose, and came out of the graves after His resurrection, and went into the holy city, and appeared unto many."

[5] Cp. footnote 13 on page 65.

Whatever other meaning one may assign to it, I am persuaded that Eph. 4.8 does not affirm the hypothesis that the naked souls of all deceased believers have been and are still being translated upwards to the glory of heaven upon death. Future resurrection and/or rapture are the prior necessities, as was the case with our Lord Jesus.

2 Corinthians 5

A third objection arises from something that Paul wrote to the Corinthian saints: "…while we are at home in the body we are absent from the Lord…but we are confident and willing, rather, to be absent from the body and to be present with the Lord" (2 Cor. 5.6b,8). This passage in no way unarguably posits that disembodied souls ascend to heaven to be with Christ personally when they die.

King David declared, "If I ascend to heaven, You are there; if I make my bed in sheol [Hades], behold, You are there" (Psa. 139.8). These comforting words, "You are there," were doubtless on Paul's mind when he assured the believers in Ephesus as follows.

> Eph. 4.9,10   In saying, "He ascended"—what does it mean except that He also had descended into the lower parts of the earth? 10 He who descended is also the One who ascended far above all the heavens, in order that He might fill all things" [This "filling" must include the lower Paradise discussed in Chapter 7].

While Christ is now bodily seated at the right hand of the Father in the Heavenly Paradise, He is surely present in Spirit even in the lower Paradise—a presence which I presume is more acutely perceived by those at rest therein than is our present experience of His indwelling our physical body.

I once sent the following one-line e-mail to a certain brother: "RIP. This acronym seems to have been better understood in centuries past than it is today."

Concerning the Ages

The N.T. reveals distinctions between ages of time as follows: ages past; this present age; an age to come (the Millennial Age); and ages unnumbered to follow thereafter into eternity's future. In order to establish this fact, and to confirm the veracity of the affirmation put forth in the Proposition appearing in Chapter 8, page 72, the following supports are being provided.

Aion

The Greek word *aion* (pronounced, ahee-ohn′)—as I understand how the N.T. employs its use with respect to time—means: "a (separate) period of time, not necessarily determinable as to its length, but set apart and distinguished from any other period of time by some certain, unique characteristic." This Greek word gives rise to the translation of the words "age" or (sometimes) "ages" in the N.T. It is through examining the various appearances of *aion* in the Greek texts, in its singular and plural number, that one is able to discover important age-distinctions being made in Scripture.

The word *aion*, in both its singular and plural number, appears more than one-hundred and twenty times in the N.T. Greek texts. Regrettably, it is oftentimes mistranslated (e.g., as "world") or even omitted in our English translations. At other times its significance is obscured through translation by its being rendered as "forever" or "forever and ever." I will deal with this last point near our end.

Baptists, Congregationalists, Presbyterians, Catholics, and Pentecostals each hold to doctrines with which the others disagree. However, if the apostles John, Paul, Peter, James and Jude had gotten together in the same room during the first century A.D., I venture to say that they would have had no disagreement over any doctrine of the faith. This is because there is one faith that has been once and for all time delivered to the saints, and we are charged to contend for its united truth for the profit of all (Jude 3).

We will begin by investigating what Scripture discloses concerning separate ages past and into this present age.

Ages Past to Present

The heavens and earth had a beginning; this is the Bible's opening declaration. But the earth created in Gen. 1.1 was found to be "without form and void"—an utter ruin—in Gen. 1.2 (cp. Jer. 4.23). However, Isa. 45.18 assures us that God did not originally create the earth in this condition; it became ruined after its original creation. Second Peter 3.5f seems to be reflecting on the earth's earlier state of ruin (in Gen. 1.2) when the apostle notes that the previous world that had existed perished.[1] So, there was at least one age of time that existed between Gen. 1.1 and 1.2.[2]

However, before there ever was an earth there were hosts of angelic beings, created by God in a previous age of time; for we are told in Job 38.4-7 that all the angels ("sons of God") were present and shouted for joy when God originally laid the foundations of the earth. Surely, then, there was at least one age of time prior Gen. 1.1. That

---

[1] This word "perish" (Greek, *apollumi*) does not mean "to cease to exist"; it means "being utterly ruined and useless as to its intended purpose."

[2] I can highly recommend a work by G. H. Pember entitled *Earth's Earliest Ages* (Kregel Publications, available from Schoettle Publishing) wherein the author discusses time prior to Gen. 1.2—time possibly consisting of billions of years.

angelic age, plus the age between Gen. 1.1 and 1.2, account for at least two ages that existed before the establishment of our present heaven-and-earth age—its re-formation being described beginning in Gen. 1.3.

These two previous ages differed in that the first age had no earth, while the second one did. Our present age is separately distinguished by the presence of man; for Scripture nowhere hints that man ever existed prior to this present age.[3]

To this point, we have discovered at least three separate ages referenced in the Bible.

Paul and the writer of Hebrews refer to ages (plural) in several places. In 1 Cor. 2.7 Paul writes, "But we speak the wisdom of God in a mystery, even the hidden wisdom, which God ordained before the ages unto our glory."[4] This wisdom originated within the Godhead before there ever was an age of time—before anything or anyone was, except God. But God's wisdom and purpose were fully revealed by the apostle Paul in Eph. 3.8f and Col. 1.25f. Other references to ages (plural) can be found in the Greek text of Heb. 1.2; 9.26; 11.3.

The conclusion of the matter, so far, is this. Not less than three distinct ages, past to present, can be identified in Scripture; and their differences as separate periods of time—each distinguished from the others by some unique characteristic—have been noted.

This Age

In all of its singular appearances in the Greek N.T., the word *aion*, when it refers to time during "this age," has only the centuries or millennia of our present age in view. When one reads Luke 1.70, John

---

[3] By "man" I mean one formed out of the dust of a refashioned earth to become a living soul when God breathed the breath of life into him (Gen. 2.7).

[4] In 1 Cor. 2.7, the word is "ages" (*aion*), and not "world" (*kosmos*). The word *aion* is erroneously rendered in many translations as "world" or "worlds." Incorrect renderings of *aion* have led to a veiling of truth when one is reading his or her own N.T.

9.32, and Acts 3.21 and 15.18, he or she should understand that the word "world" or "time" is actually *aion*, "age"; but, again, in these verses the word *aion* has only to do with time during our present age.[5]

The term "this age" often has time itself in view.[6] But, and as an aside, time alone is not always the writer's focus when "this age" appears in our English N.T. *Aion* is sometimes an important notice of the ungodly, worldly influences that bear upon men in this present age.

Concerning the use of *aion* in this sense, Paul admonishes believers: "Be not conformed to this age, but be transformed by the renewing of your mind" (Rom. 12.2). He elsewhere says that Christ was sacrificed for our sins in order that "He might rescue us from this present, evil age" (Gal. 1.4). Paul further reminds believers of how we used to walk "according to the course *[the ways]* of this world:" literally it reads, "the age *[aion]* of this world *[kosmos]*" (Eph. 2.2).[7]

In other verses, "this age" has reference to a preoccupation with or a love of the allurements of this worldly age. Paul says in one place: "Demas, having loved this present age *[aion]*, has deserted me...."[8]

Aion is also used with reference to the foolishness of the so called wise disputers of this age.[9]

---

[5] In the context of Luke 1.67-75, there is a restricting of the word *aion* (v.70)—when Zacharias is prophesying about God's holy prophets "from of old" (NASB), or "long ago" (NIV)—to include only time since the creation of man in this age. For while the Bible presents a few shrouded histories of time prior to Gen. 1.3, no prophecy previous to our present age (except one originating from God alone) ever appears in Scripture. This same reasoning also applies to the references in John and Acts.

[6] E.g., Matt. 12.32; Mark 10.30; Luke 18.30; Luke 20.34f; Eph. 1.21; Jude 25. It is of interest to note that the Greek text of each of these footnoted references directly contrasts this present time or age with either a future age or the ages to come. This age is unique when compared to those ages, as we shall see.

[7] This literal rendering is a part of the translations of Darby, EMTV, YLT, and NASB (margin).

[8] 2 Tim. 4.10; cp. 1 Tim. 6.17ff; Titus 2.12—the Greek is *aion*, not *kosmos*.

[9] 1 Cor. 1.20; and see 1 Cor. 2.6,8; 3.18.

Spiritual rulers of darkness hold sway over the affairs of men in this age.[10]

Jesus spoke about "the care *[the anxiety]* of this age and the deceitfulness of its riches."[11]

In the Parable of the Unjust Steward, Jesus contrasts the worldly wisdom of "the sons of this age" *[viz., the unrighteous, unsaved ones]* with what ought to be the spiritual wisdom of "the sons of light" *[viz., God's redeemed ones]*; these latter ones are frequently and comparatively unwise in attending to their future destiny (Luke 16.1ff).

While we have discovered that the term "this age" is not always limited to being a reference to time alone, our focus in what follows will be on the word *aion* where time is the specific thing in view.

The End of the Age

The verses noticed in this section have reference to the end of the days of this age: those which began in Adam's time and will continue in increasing wickedness unto their conclusion. As previously noted in Chapter 7, even the prophet Daniel was informed of this end more than five hundred years before Christ first came.

> Dan. 12.1-13 …13 But as for you *[Daniel]*, go your way till the end *[viz., the end of your life]*; then you will enter into rest *[in Paradise]* and *[then]* rise again *[in the resurrection of the just]* for your allotted portion *[in the kingdom]* at the end of the days *[the end of these present days: "the end of the age" in the NASB]*.

Jesus was asked by certain disciples concerning the end of the age in Matt. 24.3, and He gave them the answers.[12] In Matt. 13.37ff, Jesus speaks (parabolically) about the separation and judgment that will ac-

---

[10] 2 Cor. 4.3,4; Eph. 6.12.

[11] Matt. 13.22; Mark 4.19.

[12] Cp. Matt. 13.37ff; 24.13ff; Mark 13.13ff.

company this end. Upon His return at the end of this age "the times of restoration of all things about which God spoke by the mouth of His holy prophets" will be ushered in (Acts 3.20f).

All Christians are in agreement that this present, sin-filled age will see its end.

That Age—The Age to Come

As we begin this section, let us briefly review a few things mentioned in earlier places and then move into a discussion of the age to come.

While an earthly kingdom message is a prominent feature in the O.T., the kingdom of heaven and the hope of its glory remained primarily a mystery until its unveiling in the N.T.[13] The nearness of this heavenly kingdom was first announced by John the Baptist, and then by Jesus.[14] Since Jesus' ascension, the kingdom's unseen presence has continued until now in the ministration of the Holy Spirit within and among believers; this was and remains a principal teaching of Jesus and His apostles. However, the splendorous appearance of Christ's kingdom will not become manifest until His return in glory.

All are agreed that eternity is forever and ever. And as we shall see, Scripture often uses the Greek word *aion* in its plural number when referring to the innumerable ages of eternity's future. However, the following passages make reference to a certain, coming age: a singular age of time to follow upon this present one. And because both Amills and Postmills posit that eternity is to commence immediately after the conclusion of this age and the resurrection of all the dead, I must wonder what age they deem the following excerpts to have in view.

> Mark 10.29,30 So Jesus answered and said, "Assuredly, I say to you, there is no one who has left house or brothers or sisters or father or mother or wife or

---

[13] Rom. 8.19ff; Col. 1.26f; 1 Thess. 2.12.

[14] Matt. 3.2; 4.17.

children or lands, for My sake and the gospel's, 30 who shall not receive a hundredfold now in this time, houses and brothers and sisters and mothers and children and lands, with persecutions; and in the age to come, eternal life." *[Parallel passage: Luke 18.29f.]*

Luke 20.34-36 Jesus said to [His antagonists], "The sons of this age marry and are given in marriage, 35 but the ones considered worthy to attain that age[15] and the resurrection from the dead, neither marry nor are given in marriage; 36 for they cannot even die anymore, because they are like angels, and are sons of God, being sons of the resurrection."

Eph. 1.20,21 [God] raised [Jesus] from the dead and seated Him at His right hand in the heavenly places, 21 far above all principality and power and might and dominion, and every name that is named, not only in this age, but also in the coming *one [singular]*.

Heb. 6.4-6 For *it is* impossible for those once having been enlightened, and having tasted of the heavenly gift, and becoming sharers of *the* Holy Spirit, 5 and tasting *the* good Word of God, and *the* works of power of *the* coming age, 6 and having fallen away, to renew *them* into repentance, *seeing that they are* again crucifying to themselves the Son of God, and are putting *Him* to open shame.

As noticed earlier, each age is differentiated from any other age by some unique characteristic. The age to come will be distinguished by a manifestation of resurrected sons and daughters of God, conformed to the image of our resurrected, glorified Lord.[16] Satan opposes this plan.

Concerning Satan's opposition I would add a bit more. Because these glorified saints will replace angelic authorities, and judge them

---

[15] In verse 35, the Greek phrase *toú aioónos ekeínou* reveals an intensified reference to "that age"—something unrecognizable in our English translation. It is curious to notice just how many commentators will not touch these verses (34-36), wherein "this age" and "that age" are succinctly and distinctly contrasted.

[16] Rom. 8.18f; Phil. 3.20f.

and the world (1 Cor. 6.2f), Satan and his imps are bent on delaying the day of ripening of believers through persecuting and/or beguiling them. Some Christians will abandon their identification as believers; others will be lulled into a spiritual sleep.[17] Please realize, beloved, that "we do not wrestle against flesh and blood, but against principalities, against powers, against the rulers of the darkness of this age, against spiritual *forces* of wickedness [or, evil] in the heavenly *places*" (Eph. 6.12).

The Ages to Come

Up to this point we have examined ages past; this age (and its end); and the next (single) age to come—the Millennium.

However, Paul informs us that there is not merely one age to follow upon this present age, but many—"that in the ages to come He might show the exceeding riches of His grace in *His* kindness toward us in Christ Jesus" (Eph. 2.7). While the N.T. has much to say about this age and the one to come, very little is made known about future ages which will follow these two.

Let us now consider the Greek phrases that underlie the terms translated as "forever" and "forever and ever" in the N.T.

Forever

The word "forever" appears many times in our English N.T. When we come across this word in any writing, we often tend to think of a long, even everlasting time. However, when "forever" is rendered from a Greek phrase that includes the singular appearance of *aion*, this word never has reference to eternity, as is commonly assumed.

I will first include some two dozen references where, in the Greek phrase in which *aion* appears in its singular number, the phrase is

---

[17] Satan is determined to steal, kill, and destroy (John 10.10); to beguile (2 Cor. 11.2f); to deceive (2 Pet. 2.1f); to persecute (Matt. 5.11f; John 15.20; Acts 14.22; 2 Thess. 1.4ff; 2 Tim. 3.12); to lull some into a spiritual sleep (1 Thess. 5.6ff); to draw some apart unto falling away (Matt. 24.24; 2 Thess. 2.3f).

rendered as "forever" in many English translations. I will italicize and parenthesize what I understand the Greek phrase to mean in each case.

The Singular Appearances of Aion as Forever

The word "forever"—when rendered from the Greek phrase *eis tón aioóna*—should be understood to mean *into the (separate, single) age (to come)*. This phrase identifies only one future age; it does not have ages (plural) or eternity in view. This Greek phrase appears in the verses footnoted below,[18] wherein it intends the meaning just given.

Three other verses in the Greek text contain the singular use of *aion* in the phrase *eis [tón] aioóna*: meaning *into an age* or *into [the] age*, though this Greek phrase is either omitted or translated as "forever" in 1 Pet. 1.23; 2 Peter 2.17; Jude 13.

A most interesting occurrence of *aion* in its singular number is found in a phrase recorded in the Greek text of Peter's second epistle, and also rendered as "forever." Its English translation is as follows.

> 2 Pet. 3.18 But grow in grace and knowledge of our Lord and Savior, Jesus Christ. To Him *be* the glory, both now and forever. Amen.

The Greek phrase underlying "forever," here in Second Peter, is *eis heeméran aioónos*. This phrase is less correctly translated as "to a day of eternity" by Darby, LITV, WNT, NASB, RSV, and most incorrectly as "on that eternal day" in the ISV. YLT translates it as, "into a day of an age." Some may allow this Greek phrase to mean "into a day-age"; and, if this is accepted, the more curious reader may be interested to compare this "day-age" possibility with 2 Pet. 3.8.

In all of these references we see the singular use of *aion* to be magnifying only the next, single, temporal age to come; in none of them should *aion* be taken to mean "eternity."

---

[18] Matt. 21.19; Mark 11.14; Luke 1.55; John 6.51,58; 8.35; 12.34; 13.8; 14.16; 1 Cor. 8.13; 2 Cor. 9.9; Heb. 5.6; 6.20; 7.17,21,24,28; 1 Pet. 1.25; 1 John 2.17; 2 John 2.

The Plural Appearances of Aion as Forever

The following references find the Greek word *aion* appearing as a plural number, *aioónas*. In its plural form, *aion* can be properly understood to mean "forever" (*an unending number of ages*, or *"eternal[ly]"*). More than half a dozen verses rightly allow such an understanding.

1. The Greek phrase *eis toús aioónas* means *into the (coming) ages*; its appearances are footnoted below.[19]

2. The phrase *eis pántas toús aioónas*, meaning *into all of the ages (to come)*, is found in Jude 25.

When all of the Greek phrases above are translated simply as "forever" in the N.T., the distinction being made in the Greek between a single "age," and "ages" plural is obscured; these words are not synonymous in any language. When uninformed of the underlying Greek, the reader of English Scripture will be unaware that distinctions do exist.

Forever and Ever

Certainly, for ease of reading, the phrase "forever and ever," where it commonly occurs, is most allowable. But again, as was the case with the word "forever," the phrase "forever and ever" tends to conceal from the reader of English what is disclosed in the Greek.

Aion—Both Singular and Plural

In Ephesians we have an example of where the word *aion* appears in both its singular and its plural number in the same phrase, (though the verse in which they appear is mistranslated in certain English texts).

> Eph. 3.21 to Him *be* the glory in the assembly and in Christ Jesus, into all the generations forever and ever.[20]

---

[19] Luke 1.33; Rom. 1.25; 9.5; 11.36; 16.27; 2 Cor. 11.31; Heb. 13.8; 1 Pet. 5.11.

[20] The correct rendering of the conclusion of Eph. 3.21 should read "...generations [geneás] forever and ever"; it is not "...ages [aion] forever and ever."

Where Eph 3.21 reads "into all the generations forever and ever," the underlying Greek is, *eis pásas tás geneás toú aioónos toón aioónoon*: viz., *into all of the generations of the (single, separate) age of the ages (plural, to come).* Here it is plain to see that one specific, future age (the Millennial Age) is being singled out from among the innumerable ages that lie in the future.

Plural Appearances of Aion as Forever and Ever

In all other cases (with one exception noted), "forever and ever" is a translation of the Greek phrase *eis toús aioónas toón aioónoon*, which phrase I understand to mean *into (all of) the ages of the (innumerable) ages (to come).* Here, *aion* twice appears in its plural number, thereby being properly understood to be a reference to the innumerable ages to follow upon this present age. This specific Greek phrase underlies the translations of "forever and ever" in the verses footnoted below.[21]

Objections

I realize that there are those who will cavil at this scrutinization of the Greek texts. They may dismiss my observations as being much to do about nothing, or claim that these unique Greek phrases are all idioms meaning (simply) "forever" or "forever and ever." They might protest that none in the earliest Church would have been aware of any distinctions, though I wonder how they may assume this to be the case; for those Christians were undoubtedly more familiar with apostolic language (writings) than are nearly all present-day readers of translations.

Furthermore, their objections seem odd in light of the fact that many academic students of Scripture are often quick to point out other particular details in the Greek text in support of what they understand to be a more correct interpretation of certain passages. They do this in

---

[21] Gal. 1.5; Phil. 4.20; 1 Tim. 1.17; 2 Tim. 4.18; Heb. 13.21; 1 Pet. 4.11; Rev. 1.6,18; 4.9,10; 5.13,14; 7.12; 10.6; 11.15; 14.11 (*eis aioónas aioónoon—into [separate] ages of [many] ages*); 15.7; 19.3; 20.10; 22.5.

order to confirm that their own considered opinion is more correct than that of another as they "earnestly contend for the faith which was once for all delivered unto the saints" (Jude 3).

Our principal focus in this chapter has been on *aion*'s reference with respect to time. But confusion comes in when both the singular rendering of *aion* as "age" and its plural rendering as "ages" are indistinguishable in our N.T. Is there nothing to be gleaned from investigating the variations in the Greek words and phrases that are the foundation of our English Bibles?—for what our translations may obscure, the Greek makes clear.

Despite the protests of some, it seems unarguable that the Greek text is explicit in recording distinctions between the singular use of *aion* (age) and its plural use (ages)—which words, in any language, are never nonchalantly interchanged.

Conclusions

Many readers may have likely found some things hard to understand in this Appendix. I empathize with them. Even so, I have purposed to cover this subject in detail and at length for these reasons.

1. To establish the veracity of my earlier Proposition in Chapter 8, page 72

2. To disclose the fact that the N.T. makes clear distinctions between the following:

   a.   separate ages past

   b.   the/this present age

   c.   that separate age to come

   d.   more ages to follow thereafter, forever and ever

Clearly, "the age to come," "the Millennium," and "that age" are equivalent terms. Will any reader, after carefully considering all that has been presented above, be able to accept the notion that "that age"

1. is a "present..." or "realized millennium," something coincident with "this age" (as per the Amill position); or that it is

2. "a millennial era"—a long period of time—yet to be unfurled in future years of "this present age" (as per the Postmill position); or that

3. "the age to come" is somehow a synonym for the innumerable "ages to come" in the future?

It is clearly none of these, and I suggest that the documentation presented herein undermines such assumptions.

Please forgive me in sounding redundant when I say, "The Millennial Age is a separate, temporal age that will commence upon the return of the Lord Jesus Christ at the end of 'this age;' and that 'that age' will be followed by innumerable ages forever and ever."

I pray that this truth concerning the Millennial Age has been opened up to you, beloved, and that we may all be "loving" and "looking for the appearing of the glory of our great God and Savior Jesus Christ," being "ready," in hope of becoming "joint heirs with Christ... glorified together with Him" in His coming kingdom.[22]

"Even so, come, Lord Jesus!" (Rev. 22.20)

---

[22] 2 Tim. 4.8...Titus 2.13...Matt. 24.44...Rom. 8.17.

A Word of Personal Testimony

My brother Bill and I were compelled by our mother to attend Sunday school throughout our adolescent years. Nevertheless, my thoughts and secret behavior were and remained godless and vile. But around age eleven certain questions began to arise in my mind—questions like, "Who is God?" "Why am I here?" and "What may happen to me when I die?" (These are questions that come into the mind of every person at some time in their life; and this is so according to the grace of God.)

Thinking that I might find some answers in the Sunday morning church services, I began attending them voluntarily and regularly. But after listening to a lot of moral platitudes and glib (often anecdotal) preachings for many months, my hope of finding any answers was dashed. So, I left off church-going and remained skeptical and unconverted for more than the next two decades of my life.

Throughout my teenage years and into my middle adulthood I became increasingly exercised in many of the vices of those who walk in the lusts of human nature and in spiritual darkness; and my companions were, for the most part, of the same bent.

When I was thirty-three years old, around Easter time, while flipping through the TV channels, I happened upon the beginning of an old black and white version of the movie, *Jesus of Nazareth*. I only intended to watch it briefly, being generally familiar with the story from my younger days. However, I soon found myself thoroughly absorbed in it.

By the time it ended, the following question had already intruded itself upon my mind: "Why did Jesus, having done so many miracles, even to the raising of the dead…why, when they unjustifiably nailed him to a cross, did he not just exercise the power that he had and come down from there to prove to his enemies who he was?" This thought revisited me on numerous occasions over the next eighteen months.

In that season of my life my already troubled personal life, including my marriage and my professional career, had deteriorated into such shambles that I suffered a nervous breakdown. The psychiatrist whom I then visited—a man three times married and divorced—proved to be of no help; so I quit him. (The blind lead the blind into a ditch [Matt. 15.14].)

During that short period of therapy, while driving home from the doctor's office one evening, I had a revelation: viz., that all of my problems were a result of reaping what I was sowing. (I had no idea at the time that this is a principle recorded throughout the Bible.)

Wanting to become a better person, I tried to reform my ways. Constant failure over the next many months made me realize that I was a captive of my sinful thoughts and deeds, and incapable of reforming them. I began to fear that if I died in this wretched and hopeless condition, I was going to stand in judgment before God—a God I knew nothing about—and I was afraid that He would send me to hell.

I was in this deplorable state of mind when my wife and I flew from our home in Connecticut to Honolulu in August, 1977. It was there that I was scheduled to take the Hawaii State Board Dental Examination. I had recently turned thirty-five years old.

We checked into our hotel room in Waikiki about seven p.m. My wife fell fast asleep; she was still on East coast time where it was one a.m. As for me…I was wide awake.

Idle curiosity led me to look into the nightstand drawer where I discovered a copy of the *Good News Bible*. After sitting and gazing at its cover for a few moments, I bowed my head and prayed something like this: "O God, you know that I'm not what you would call a Christian, though I have known some things about Jesus since my childhood. But I think the time has come for me to find out just what it is concerning this man that has caused millions of people to trust and believe in him. So, I'm going to read this Bible, and I pray that you will reveal to me whatever it is that I need to know. Thank you. Amen."

I began reading the book of Matthew, and I soon found myself spellbound by it. In fact, as I can vividly recall, the printer's ink was lifting off of the pages of that Bible, the words floating into my mind and into my heart. The narratives of Jesus' godly life, his miracles, his teachings, and especially the fact that he had an answer for every question that his enemies attempted to entangle him in…all of these accounts were becoming credible and believable to me.

While I was reading about his crucifixion, God suddenly revealed to me why this powerful miracle-worker would not save himself from the unimaginably horrific torment of scourging and crucifixion; I realized that while I deserved to be punished, this godly, righteous man was suffering in my place!

In tears, I turned the page. And there I read the words of an angel spoken to certain women who had come to Jesus' (empty) tomb. "He is risen!" declared the angel. When I read those words on that night I believed them! In those same moments Life seemed to be gushing into me, and I felt the huge burden of my hopelessness being lifted away. I actually had a hope for the first time in my life—hope that because Jesus Christ was raised from the dead, I would live also. (To live, and not to die condemned…this is what a man really wants, is it not?)

Finally, I had been brought to a living faith in Jesus; I had been born again. I had come to believe the truth: that Jesus Christ is the crucified, resurrected Son of God, and a Savior for all who receive Him.

My wife and I left Hawaii to return home about ten days later. Several days after our return I made my first confession of faith—to my wife. She, having been a believer since her childhood, cried with joy.

The next thing I wanted to do, after my twenty-plus-year truancy, was to go to church. Because there was one just a block south of our house, the following Sunday my wife and I gathered up our children and went right down there. And when we opened up those hymnals on that morning, I opened my mouth wide and sang out with a loud voice and a joyful heart.

3747430R00111

Printed in Great Britain
by Amazon.co.uk, Ltd.,
Marston Gate.